Does *Traditionis Custodes* Pass the Juridical Rationality Test?

Os Justi Studies in Catholic Tradition

—⁓—

Fr. Réginald-Marie Rivoire, F.S.V.F.

Does *Traditionis Custodes* Pass the Juridical Rationality Test?

A Canonical-Theological Study

Translated by
Fr. William Barker, F.S.S.P.

Post-Rescript Revised Edition

OS JUSTI PRESS

Lincoln, Nebraska

Cover design: Julian Kwasniewski

Cover image: Adobe stock 35861260—stock.adobe.com

Os Justi Press
Lincoln, NE
https://osjustipress.com/

Inquiries to
info@osjustipress.com

ISBN 979-8-36280-463-3

Nihil obstat
Rev. Fr. Joseph-Marie GILLIOT, f. s. v. f.
Rev. Fr. Augustin-Marie AUBRY, f. s. v. f.

Imprimi potest
Rev. Fr. Louis-Marie DE BLIGNIÈRES, f. s. v. f.
Prior of the Saint-Vincent-Ferrier Fraternity
Chémeré-le-Roi, March 7, 2023, feast of Saint Thomas Aquinas

This work is the updated and expanded version of an article published in *Spiritu Ferventes, Mélanges en l'honneur de l'abbé Bernard Lucien à l'occasion de son 70e anniversaire* (Poitiers: DMM, 2022)

Contents

Note on the Translation

Where Fr. Rivoire cites a Church document in French, we use herein the official English translation from the Vatican website, whenever available. Works quoted in various languages for which no published English translation exists or could be located were translated directly from Fr. Rivoire's text, with their titles left in the original languages.

Introduction

On July 16, 2021, the feast of Our Lady of Mount Carmel, Pope Francis published *Traditionis Custodes*[1] (*TC*), an Apostolic Letter given *motu proprio*, drastically restricting the use of the traditional Roman liturgy. The use of the 1962 *Missale Romanum* is now subject to the authorization of the diocesan bishop (art. 5), who must himself consult the Apostolic See before granting the same to a newly ordained priest (art. 4). It is also up to the bishop to

---

[1] The only part of document which is in Latin is its title—an anomaly that has become anything but rare under the current pontificate. The original version is in Italian. This is the version that was promulgated by its publication in *L'Osservatore Romano*. This Italian text *alone* is the authentic and prevailing version, unless otherwise indicated in the yet-to-be publication in the *Acta Apostolicæ Sedis*, in which case we would be dealing with a new law and a new promulgation. Here we will quote the official English translations of the *motu proprio* and of the accompanying Letter as found on the Vatican website.

determine the days and places where Mass may be celebrated publicly according to the 1962 Missal—and this must in any case be outside parish churches (art. 3). Moreover, the bishop must be careful to not authorize the creation of any new groups (art. 3 §5), and even less erect new personal parishes (art. 3 §2); instead, he is encouraged to verify that existing personal parishes are "effective for the spiritual growth [of the faithful]" (art. 3 §5). The "Fourth Section" of the Congregation for the Doctrine of the Faith, heir to the Pontifical Commission *Ecclesia Dei*, which was responsible for matters pertaining to the *usus antiquior* as well as for Institutes entirely dedicated to its celebration, is *de facto* suppressed. These Institutes come under the purview of the Congregation for Institutes of Consecrated Life and Societies of Apostolic Life (art. 6), whereas the Congregation for Divine Worship and the Discipline of the Sacraments becomes competent for the relevant liturgical matters (art. 7).[2] Finally, the pope makes it clear that previous norms, instructions, concessions, and usages that are not in conformity with the provisions of his new motu proprio are abrogated (art. 8).

In a letter to the bishops published on the same day, the Holy Father explains at length the reasons for his decision. The expressions used are marked by a virulence that was thought to have disappeared from papal documents, at least since "the Bride of Christ prefers to make use of the medicine of mercy

---

[2] Since Pentecost 2022, as per the provisions of the Apostolic Constitution *Praedicate Evangelium*, these congregations are now called dicasteries.

rather than to brandish the weapons of severity."[3] Indeed, it is with difficulty that even the most casual of readers would repress the painful impression of being confronted with a series of invectives against traditionalists. It is "in defense of the unity of the Body of Christ" that Pope Francis says he is "constrained to revoke the faculty granted by [his] predecessors," speaking of a "distorted use that has been made of [it]." For the Holy Father, this faculty to use the books that preceded the liturgical reform was granted only to "provide for the good of those who are rooted in the previous form of celebration and need to return in due time to the Roman Rite promulgated by Saints Paul VI and John Paul II." In fact, this faculty has been used "to widen the gaps, reinforce the divergences, and encourage disagreements that injure the Church, block her path, and expose her to the peril of division." "[T]he instrumental use of the Missale Romanum of 1962 is often characterized by a rejection not only of the liturgical reform, but of the Vatican Council II itself, claiming, with unfounded and unsustainable assertions, that it betrayed the Tradition and the 'true Church.'" In the eyes of the Holy Father, "ever more plain in the words and attitudes of many is the close connection between the choice of celebrations according to the liturgical books prior to Vatican

---

3   John XXIII, Address on the Occasion of the Solemn Opening of the Most Holy [Second Vatican] Council, October 11, 1962, no. 7: "*ad præsens tempus quod attinet, Christi Sponsæ placet misericordiæ medicinam adhibere, potius quam severitatis arma suscipere.*"

Council II and the rejection of the Church and her institutions in the name of what is called the 'true Church.'" The pope sees in this a "comportment that contradicts communion and nurtures the divisive tendency . . . against which the Apostle Paul so vigorously reacted." As for the personal parishes that have been erected here and there in accordance with the motu proprio *Summorum Pontificum*, he believes that they are "tied more to the desire and wishes of individual priests than to the real need of the 'holy people of God.'" In short, Francis intends to put an end to what he clearly considers an *abuse of law* on the part of the beneficiaries of the faculties granted by John Paul II and Benedict XVI, and thus "re-establish unity throughout the Church of the Roman Rite," a unity which according to him is jeopardized by the use of the 1962 Missal.[4]

The surprisingly harsh measures taken by the Holy Father, together with the violent and accusatory tone of the accompanying Letter, have aroused great emotion among the faithful who are attached to that which, since the motu proprio *Summorum Pontificum* of Benedict XVI, had been known as "the Extraordinary Form of the Roman Rite." At the same time, the inaccuracies, the difficulties of interpretation and of concrete application of the recent motu proprio, have raised many questions among canonists, pastors, and institutes whose proper law binds them to the liturgical forms of the previous Latin tradition. This made

---

[4] In the English version, the word "unity" appears seventeen times in the letter, and the word "communion" six times.

it necessary to quickly publish an implementation document. Accordingly, on December 18, 2021, the Congregation for Divine Worship and the Discipline of the Sacraments (hereafter CDW) published the "*Responsa ad dubia* on some provisions of the Apostolic Letter issued *motu proprio Traditionis custodes.*"[5] It is to be feared, however, that these "responses" raise, in turn, more difficulties than they resolve.

This tract is intended as a canonical reading of those documents, chiefly from the point of view of their rationality. It is well known that rationality is one of the essential characteristics of a legal norm, such that, strictly speaking, an irrational norm is not a norm and does not bind.[6]

We shall first briefly consider the legal status of these documents (chapter 1). Then, we shall study at length the affirmation that is at the heart of this whole legal apparatus and its *raison d'être*, namely, that the liturgical books promulgated by Paul VI and John Paul II are the sole expression of the *lex orandi* of the

---

[5] Congregation for Divine Worship and the Discipline of the Sacraments, "*Responsa ad Dubia* on Some Provisions of the Apostolic Letter Issued *motu proprio Traditionis Custodes* of the Supreme Pontiff Francis," December 4, 2021.

[6] Cf. St. Thomas Aquinas, *Sum. theol.*, Ia-IIae, q. 90, a. 4: "The law is nothing other than a certain ordination of reason, with a view to the common good, promulgated by one who has charge of the community (*quædam rationis ordinatio ad bonum commune, et ab eo qui curam communitatis habet, promulgata*)." As a consequence, "a tyrannical law, since it is not according to reason, is not strictly speaking a law, but rather a perversion of law (*lex tyrannica, cum non sit secundum rationem, non est simpliciter lex, sed magis est quædam perversitas legis*)" (*Sum. theol.*, Ia-IIæ, q. 92, a. 1, ad 4).

Roman Rite (chapter 2). Finally, we will see how numerous fundamental principles of canon law are undermined by these new norms (chapter 3). We will then try to draw some conclusions as to what might be the future of this legislation (chapter 4).

1

The Juridical Nature of the Documents

~~~∂σ~~~

The Motu Proprio

This motu proprio is the thirty-seventh such document of Pope Francis, who since his election to the See of Peter has displayed an uncommon legislative activity[7] that has generated perplexity and uneasiness among canonists of all tendencies—at least those who do not profess to be courtiers.[8]

---

[7] It could perhaps only be compared, in modern times, with that of Paul VI in the years following the Second Vatican Council. A quick look at the Holy See's website reveals that between the beginning of his pontificate on March 13, 2013, and July 16, 2021, Pope Francis has promulgated no less than four Apostolic Constitutions, thirty-seven motu proprios, and eleven laws and statutes concerning entities of the Holy See or Vatican City, not to mention numerous chirographs and audience rescripts of a legislative nature. Within a similar timeframe (eight years), Benedict XVI issued only one Apostolic Constitution and thirteen motu proprios.

[8] On Francis as legislator, and in particular on the sidelining, during his pontificate, of the Pontifical Council for Legislative Texts—the Dicastery specially in

Does *Traditionis Custodes* Pass the Juridical Rationality Test?

It has been surprisingly claimed that this motu proprio is act of the pope's *magisterium*.[9] In and of itself, a motu proprio is not an act of magisterial power, but a papal *law* and therefore an act of the power of jurisdiction. Unlike Apostolic Constitutions, which are generally laws reforming an entire subject, the genre of motu proprio[10] is used by the Supreme Pontiffs to issue

---

charge of providing technical and juridical expertise to the Supreme Pontiff and the Roman Curia in the elaboration of universal norms—see Geraldina Boni, *La recente attività normativa ecclesiale: finis terræ per lo* ius canonicum? *Per una valorizzazione del ruolo del Pontificio Consiglio per i testi legislativi e della scienza giuridica nella Chiesa* (Modena: Mucchi Editore, 2021). The author's observations are severe: "Legislation is currently being handed down in the Church, because legislative stasis is unthinkable; yet it is being legislated plethorically and hypertrophically—marriage, tribunal, measures of sanction, the Roman Curia, economics and finance, etc.—and unfortunately almost always without due skillfulness or mastery [of the law]" (178). Further: "If the provisions, drafted without appropriate legal terminology and coherence with the legal order, create doubts and problems instead of resolving them—if they disturb, so to speak, the *tranquillitas ordinis* and severely wound the rights and expectations of the faithful—there ends up lacking in them that *rationabilitas* [reasonableness] without which the law is *corruptela iuris* [a corruption of law]" (266).

[9] Henry Donneaud, O.P., "Le pape François garant de la doctrine liturgique de saint Pie V," in *Nouvelle revue théologique* 144 (Jan.-March 2022), 38–54: "Thus, he carries forward the Magisterium, since he illuminates and prolongs the teaching of his predecessor" (43); "the contribution of Francis, according to the process of homogeneous doctrinal growth of the Magisterium, has as its principal motive to better guarantee the *ontological* truth of the liturgical doctrine of the Church" (45–46).

[10] The full title is *litteræ apostolicæ motu proprio datæ* ("apostolic letter given *motu proprio*"). Traditionally, the term *motu proprio* (ablative: "of his own motion," "on his own initiative") indicates that the Roman Pontiff is making provisions

or modify norms on a particular point (even if perhaps of great importance). In fact, the term does not refer to a clearly defined normative typology. In the Church, the Roman Pontiff's *plenitudo potestatis* is not bound by any formal requirements.[11] The production and emanation of legislative acts is not subject to any formal requirement *ad validitatem*. It is not, therefore, the *intitulatio* of a document which chiefly sheds light on its nature (even if this is a valuable clue), but its very content. In this case, Pope Francis, by revoking the faculties granted by his predecessors, and by subjecting celebrations according to the 1962 Missal to strict conditions, intends to establish a new general, abstract, permanent, and obligatory norm, i.e., to establish a new juridical order. In so doing, he exercises his power of jurisdiction. In itself, the motu proprio *Traditionis Custodes* is formally disciplinary, not doctrinal.

---

without there being a specific prior request (or, if there is one, without its being the reason for the law). This is what fundamentally distinguishes a motu proprio from decretal laws. Cf. José Antonio Araña, "*Motu proprio,*" in *Diccionario General de Derecho Canónico* [*DGDC*], ed. J. Otaduy, A. Viana, J. Sedano, vol. 5 (Cizur Menor/Navarra: Editorial Aranzadi, 2012), 484.

11 Obviously, this does not mean that the Roman Pontiff should disregard the legal certainty afforded by the observance of certain procedures and formalities in the elaboration of norms. Nor, even less, may he exempt himself from respect for essential and constitutive elements of juridical institutions and acts (see can. 86). For example, it is of the essence of the law that it be promulgated (see can. 7: "*Lex instituitur cum promulgatur*"), i.e., that it be publicly, authentically, and officially made known by the competent authority. That being said, provided that these essential characteristics are respected, the method of promulgation may take various forms.

This first observation is of great importance. In order to understand its significance, it is perhaps not useless to recall the doctrine of the real and specific distinction between the power of magisterium (or teaching) and the power of jurisdiction (or government) in the Church.[12] By affirming a real and specific distinction, we mean that the distinction in question is not a mere convenient classification, based on extrinsic reasons, where one power could be reduced to the other. On the contrary, the distinction here proceeds from the intrinsic formal reasons of each of the two powers. The power of magisterium has, as its formal object, revealed truth (or truth related to the revealed). Its proper act is that of teaching, and its intrinsic end is to obtain the assent of the believer's intelligence. The power of jurisdiction has, as its formal object, human acts which conduce to the end of the Church. Its act is that of commanding for the common good, and its intrinsic end is to obtain the obedience of the will.

To teach is not to command. A teaching is true or false, whereas a law is more or less prudent. The faithful's attitude towards a document of ecclesial authority is therefore fundamentally different, depending on whether the document is magisterial or disciplinary. To a teaching of the magisterium is due the assent of the intellect, according to the doctrine of the degrees of

---

[12] For further explanations, we refer to our own work: Réginald-Marie Rivoire, F.S.V.F., *La valeur doctrinale de la discipline canonique* (Rome: EDUSC, 2016), ch. II: "Deux pouvoirs distincts: magistère et juridiction," 114–64.

authority of the magisterium.[13] To a command of the power of jurisdiction, is due the obedience of the will, insofar as: (1) there is an order from a legitimate superior; (2) this superior commands in the area of his jurisdiction; (3) the order is not clearly contrary to the precept of a higher superior. If one of these three conditions is lacking, i.e., if the superior is not legitimate, or does not command within the area of his jurisdiction, or contradicts the order of a higher superior, then abuse of power takes place. In such a case, not only is the recipient not required to obey, but sometimes he or she must not do so, especially if what is commanded is sinful—since the order received then contradicts the order of the highest superior, who is God. No authority on earth has unlimited power, not even the pope.

Since the motu proprio is a pontifical law regarding a liturgical matter, it is useful to recall the limits of authority in this domain. Contrary to a widespread understanding according to which "the pope can do anything," or that "what one pope has done, another

---

[13] Cf. Second Vatican Council, Dogmatic Constitution *Lumen Gentium*, no. 25 (which emphasizes that assent must be given "according to his [the Supreme Pontiff's] manifest mind and will. His mind and will in the matter may be known either from the character of the documents, from his frequent repetition of the same doctrine, or from his manner of speaking"). On the degrees of authority of the Magisterium, see Bernard Lucien, "The Magisterial Authority of Vatican II," *Sedes Sapientiæ*, Special English-language Issue, 2022, pp. 21–90, especially ch. 2, "The Diversification of Magisterial Authority in General," 37–51. See also Augustin-Marie Aubry, F.S.V.F., *Obéir ou assentir? De la "soumission religieuse" au magistère simplement authentique* (Paris: Desclée De Brouwer, 2015) and John P. Joy, *Disputed Questions on Papal Infallibility* (Lincoln, NE: Os Justi Press, 2022).

pope can undo," it is necessary to recall that, in fact, the pope cannot "do anything." Even in disciplinary matters, he is not an absolute monarch whose will is law. This is true, first of all, because he is obviously bound to respect divine law (the divine-apostolic tradition, which in part contains discipline); but also because he is not totally above certain human apostolic or ecclesiastical traditions, which maintain a more or less strong relationship of congruency with the revealed deposit. The liturgy is the privileged domain of this intertwining of the divine, the (simply) apostolic, and the ecclesiastical. Father Yves Congar remarked:

> We can see that there is often an entanglement of what is ecclesiastical with what is divine or apostolic—an entanglement such that, as clear (and important!) as the distinction is in principle, it cannot be pushed to the limit in real life. This situation favors a global respect; it even requires it. The critical spirit finds this difficult to deal with, but, while pursuing valid and even necessary distinctions, it must understand that, in the end, this relative indistinction in fact finds its explanation in the very nature of things.[14]

"This situation favors a global respect." Such respect is also, and even primarily, required of the Supreme Pontiff. Benedict XVI stressed this in one of his first homilies:

---

[14] Yves Marie-Joseph Congar, O.P., *La Tradition et la vie de l'Église* (Paris: Fayard, 1963), 39–40. Here again we refer to our work: Rivoire, *La valeur doctrinale*, 68–76.

The pope is not an absolute monarch whose thoughts and desires are law. On the contrary: the pope's ministry is a guarantee of obedience to Christ and to his Word. He must not proclaim his own ideas, but rather constantly bind himself and the Church to obedience to God's Word, in the face of every attempt to adapt it or water it down, and every form of opportunism. . . . The pope knows that in his important decisions, he is bound to the great community of faith of all times, to the binding interpretations that have developed throughout the Church's pilgrimage. Thus, his power is not being above, but at the service of, the Word of God. It is incumbent upon him to ensure that this Word continues to be present in its greatness and to resound in its purity, so that it is not torn to pieces by continuous changes in usage.[15]

The Accompanying Letter

The purpose of the accompanying Letter is to provide information on the purpose and circumstances of the new law, as well as on the *mens legislatoris*. It does not, therefore, constitute a legal norm, nor is it binding on those to whom the law is addressed. "*Ratio legis non est ipsa lex*," as the saying goes. What counts is the objective law (the rational order effectively established, as

---

[15] Benedict XVI, Homily at Mass of Possession of the Chair of the Bishop of Rome, May 7, 2005, in *AAS* 97 (2005): 748–52.

expressed, first of all,[16] by the legal text), because the reasons provided by the legislator may go beyond what is actually established by the law or, conversely, indicate less than what is ordered. The intention of the legislator (*finis operantis*) is thus always secondary in relation to the objective end of the concrete legal ordination (*finis operis*).

Here again, it is important to guard oneself against a voluntaristic view of the law. The law is not essentially a precept of the legislator's will, but rather a rational ordering made for the common good. The legislator's motives are certainly indicative of the rational order that he intends to establish, but they should not be given a normative value that they do not have. To repeat, for example, over and over again that "the pope's wishes are orders" is to convey, under cover of a (falsely) pious formula, a voluntaristic view of the law. No, the pope's wishes are not

---

[16] We say "first of all" because we certainly do not mean to say that the mere grammatical or logical analysis of the text is sufficient to grasp the social order established by the legislator. This can be easily understood from the following example provided by Prof. Eduardo Baura (*Parte generale del diritto canonico. Diritto e sistema normativo* [Rome: EDUSC, 2013], 334–35): "In order to interpret a law governing the administration of a sacrament . . . , the most important and decisive element to be taken into consideration will be the nature of the sacrament itself, which allows us to understand what is the order established for its administration. It is not a matter of deducing said nature from the words of the law, but rather of grasping the right meaning of the words in the light of the nature of the reality being regulated: '*Non sermoni res, sed rei est sermo subjectus*' (X 5.40.6). And if, God forbid, the words of a law were to contradict the very nature of the regulated reality, such a law would be irrational and invalid."

orders. Had the legislator intended to make orders of his wishes, he would have expressed them and promulgated them as such: "*Quod voluit exprimit, quod noluit tacuit.*"[17]

For this reason, diocesan authorities may not appeal to "the concerns of the Holy Father," "the anguish of the Holy Father," or "the spirit of the legislator," in order to enforce measures which, in their severity, would go beyond the legal text. This is all the more true in light of the principle "*odiosa sunt restringenda*": "Laws which prescribe a penalty, or restrict the free exercise of rights, or contain an exception to the law, are to be interpreted strictly" (can. 18). It is therefore perfectly irrational to invoke *TC* or its accompanying Letter to prohibit the use of liturgical books that are not directly addressed by the legal text, or to limit celebrations in the *usus antiquior* to certain days only, especially if this goes against the very nature of a juridical institution. Thus, the establishment of a parish always entails the exercise, guaranteed to the faithful, of *full pastoral care* (*cura pastoralis*; cf. can. 515 §1). Although a bishop may, for a just cause assessed in a discretionary but not arbitrary manner, suppress an already erected parish[18] (cf. can. 515 §2),

---

[17] *Dig.* l. XIV, tit. I, *De exercitoria actione*, lex 1, *Utilitatem*, §20, *Licet.* We shall see the consequences of these principles when assessing whether Pope Paul VI did or did not abrogate the so-called Missal of St. Pius V. If the pope wishes to abrogate a norm, he must do so in the due form.

[18] Precedents in this matter are relatively abundant. For a recent case, cf. Supreme Tribunal of the Apostolic Signatura, October 2, 2018, Prot. n. 52094/16 CA, Ordinariato militare N. Della soppressione della parrocchia X presso l'Accademia

he may not create the juridical monster that would be a parish without Mass or without sacraments. This would be like trying to create a square circle.[19]

The *Responsa ad Dubia*

This document of the CDW, released on December 18, but dated December 4, is signed—unusually[20]—by the sole Prefect, Arthur Roche. It is presented in the form of "answers" to *dubia* (questions), accompanied by explanatory notes. The whole was approved by the Supreme Pontiff, but only in simple form, not

---

Militare Y (Rev.do Z e altri, Congregazione per il Clero), commentary by Giovanni Parise in "Soppressione di una parrocchia e impossibilità di sanare un atto amministrativo illegittimo da parte del superiore gerarchico," in *Ius Ecclesiæ* XXXIII/1 (2021): 241–74.

[19] This is, however, what the Cardinal Vicar of Rome decided in a "Pastoral Letter" dated October 7, 2021, Prot. n. 1845/21: "Tutti i giorni, *eccetto il Triduo Pasquale*, i fedeli potranno partecipare alla celebrazione eucaristica secondo il Missale Romanum del 1962 nella Parrocchia Santissima Trinità dei Pellegrini (cf. art. 3 §5, *Traditionis custodes*)." During the Triduum, the three holiest days of the liturgical year, therefore, the faithful of this personal parish are expected to go elsewhere to seek the salvific goods. Such a provision is obviously invalid, since it goes against the very nature of a parish.

[20] Article 131 §7 of the General Regulations of the Roman Curia (*Regolamento Generale della Curia Romana* [RGCR]) states that documents issued by Dicasteries must be countersigned by their Secretary. This procedure, while not being *ad validitatem*, aims to ensure the correctness of the texts (of which the Secretary is the guarantor). It was not respected in the case at hand.

in specific form.[21] The document remains, therefore, a document of the Dicastery, of a purely administrative, and not legislative, nature, since the Dicastery does not enjoy legislative power. Thus, despite its presentation (formulation of a legal doubt followed by a laconic answer: yes or no), this document is by no means an *authentic interpretation, per modum legis*. Such interpretations, which do have the force of law (and therefore must be promulgated), are legislative acts that may be enacted only by the Pontifical Council for Legislative Texts whose ordinary competence is to do so,[22] or by another Dicastery, but then with the *express* delegation of the supreme legislator (always possible under can. 135 §2).

Since the *Responsa* are not an authentic interpretation of *TC*, they are a general administrative document, issued by an executive authority, as an accessory to a law. In its own words, this document intends to provide some "clarification" on the "correct application" of the motu proprio. Canonists will therefore call these *Responsa* either a *general executory decree*[23] or an

---

21 At the end of the document's introduction, it is stated that: "The Supreme Pontiff Francis, in the course of an Audience granted to the Prefect of this Congregation on November 18, 2021, was informed of and gave his consent to the publication of these *Responsa ad Dubia* with attached Explanatory Notes."

22 Cf. Apostolic Const. *Pastor Bonus*, art. 155: "With regard to the universal laws of the Church, the Council is competent to publish authentic interpretations by pontifical authority. . . ."

23 Cf. can. 31 §1: "Within the limits of their competence, those who have executive power can issue general executory decrees, that is, decrees which define more precisely the manner of applying a law, or which urge the observance of laws."

instruction.[24] The fact that the document is addressed to the Presidents of the Episcopal Conferences, i.e., to those authorities responsible for the execution of the law (and not to all the faithful), invites one to lean towards the second qualification. In any case, regardless of whether they are a general executory decree or an instruction, the *Responsa* remain *secundum legem* and *infra legem*, i.e., subordinate to the law. Accordingly, their provisions cannot in any way contradict a law. This is the principle of the hierarchy of norms, expressed both in canon 33 §1: "General executory decrees . . . do not derogate from the law, and any of their provisions which are contrary to the law have no force," and in canon 34 §2: "The regulations of an instruction do not derogate from the law, and if there are any which cannot be reconciled with the provisions of the law they have no force."

It is precisely in order to prevent a Dicastery from taking administrative measures *præter* or *contra legem*, which would be necessarily null and void, that the *General Regulations of the Roman Curia* provide that general executory decrees or instructions emanating from a Dicastery must be sent to the Pontifical Council for Legislative Texts for prior review of their conformity

---

[24] Cf. can. 34 §1: "Instructions, namely, which set out the provisions of a law and develop the manner in which it is to be put into effect, are given for the benefit of those whose duty it is to execute the law, and they bind them in executing the law. Those who have executive power may, within the limits of their competence, lawfully publish such instructions."

with the law in force.[25] Was such review carried out for the present *Responsa ad Dubia*? The question is open to doubt, since, as we shall see, these responses openly contradict the *Code of Canon Law* on several points.[26]

---

[25] *RGCR*, art. 131 §5: "I documenti dei Dicasteri destinati alla pubblicazione ... se hanno la natura di decreti generali esecutivi o di istruzioni, devono essere inviati, per un esame circa la loro congruenza legislativa con il diritto vigente e la loro corretta forma giuridica, al Pontificio Consiglio per l'Interpretazione dei Testi Legislativi" ("documents of the Dicasteries intended for publication ... if they are in the nature of general executive decrees or instructions, must be sent, for an examination as to their legislative congruence with current law and their correct legal form, to the Pontifical Council for the Interpretation of Legislative Texts").

[26] The *Responsa* violate canons 87 §1 (the right of diocesan bishops to dispense from a universal law), 902 (priests' right not to concelebrate), 905 §2 (the possibility for any priest to "binate," with the permission of the local Ordinary). Not to mention canons 213 (the right of the faithful to receive the spiritual riches from their pastors, in particular the Word of God and the Sacraments) and 214 (the right of the faithful to worship God according to the provisions of their own rite and to follow their own form of spiritual life in accord with the doctrine of the Church).

2

A Unique Expression of the
Lex Orandi of the Roman Rite?

Two First Articles, Two Arts of Legislating

The provision of *TC* that has caused the most astonishment and has already attracted much attention is undoubtedly article 1, whereby the pope decides that "The liturgical books promulgated by Saint Paul VI and Saint John Paul II, in conformity with the decrees of Vatican Council II, are the unique expression of the *lex orandi* of the Roman Rite."

Concise as it is, this article is the exact opposite of article 1 of the motu proprio *Summorum Pontificum*, which stated:

> The Roman Missal promulgated by Pope Paul VI is the or-
> dinary expression of the *lex orandi* of the Catholic Church
> of the Latin rite. The Roman Missal promulgated by Saint

Pius V and revised by Blessed John XXIII is nonetheless to be considered an extraordinary expression of the same *lex orandi* of the Church and duly honored for its venerable and ancient usage. These two expressions of the Church's *lex orandi* will in no way lead to a division in the Church's *lex credendi*; for they are two usages of the one Roman Rite.

We find here a truly striking contrast between two manners of legislating, one marked by juridical realism, the other by voluntaristic positivism. While Benedict XVI *acknowledged*, by a *declarative* act, two ritual realities which, *de facto*, exist today in the Latin Church (one dating back to antiquity, the other to 1969), and sought to give them a juridical framework, Francis *decides*, by a *performative* act, that only one of these two realities exists in the Church, in this case the one born in 1969; the other *no longer exists*. It already no longer exists *in law*, and the legislator wills that it disappear *in fact*.[27]

---

[27] According to the Supreme Legislator, the *usus antiquior* is clearly destined to disappear, since art. 3 §6 states that the bishop should "take care not to authorize the establishment of new groups." In the accompanying Letter, it is further indicated that the faithful "need to return in due time to the Roman Rite promulgated by Saints Paul VI and John Paul II." It is therefore only a matter of time. Clearly, the long-term aim is complete suppression, and this is logical given that, according to the text, there is only "one expression" of the *lex orandi*. The pope therefore invites bishops to "proceed in such a way as to return to a unitary form of celebration (*una forma celebrativa unitaria*)."

A Unique Expression of the Lex Orandi *of the Roman Rite?*

In article 1 of *Summorum Pontificum*, the normative act is a rational one, not primarily because it is the fruit of the legislator's reasoning, but because it is measured by an objective reality that imposes itself on the legislator (indeed, reality itself does not come under his *dominium*): there are two ritual realities and the legislator intends to order them in the best way possible in view of the common good, giving them a juridical name (ordinary or extraordinary "form" of the Roman Rite), and a corresponding juridical regime. One might discuss the choice of this innovative terminology and the juridical regime attached thereto, but one cannot deny that the pope has exercised legislative prudence.

In article 1 of *TC*, on the other hand, the normative act, certainly preceded—one would hope—by reasoning, appears more as an act of the will of the legislator. The logic followed is normativistic and legalistic, which is not only inappropriate in itself, but seems particularly unsuited to the field of liturgy that it claims to regulate: a Missal is not the highway code. What is shocking is not so much that Francis contradicts his predecessor, but that he treats a liturgical rite of many centuries' standing as if it were a purely disciplinary matter. Certainly, this kind of normativistic view applied to the liturgy is not limited to Pope Francis. The same logic was at work in the liturgical reform of Paul VI. The latter observation is important and deserves some attention.

Article 1 of *TC* states that "the liturgical books promulgated by Saint Paul VI and Saint John Paul II" are "in conformity with the decrees of the Vatican Council II." This claim is questionable. In fact, it has been amply demonstrated that the Missal of Paul VI went far beyond the conciliar mandate, creating a liturgy *ex novo*, in discontinuity not only with the tradition represented by the Missal of St. Pius V, but also with the very will of the Conciliar Fathers.

The Rite of Paul VI is Not
the Mass Called for by Vatican II

The Mass of Paul VI goes far beyond the prescriptions of *Sacrosanctum Concilium* (*SC*). Nowhere, for example, did the Council envisage the abolition of the traditional offertory, the composition of new Eucharistic prayers, the abolition or modification of almost all prayers,[28] the celebration of Mass facing the people, the recitation of the Canon in a loud voice, or the distribution

---

[28] As research demonstrates, "a mere 13% (165) of the 1,273 prayers of the *usus antiquior* found their way unchanged into the reformed Missal of Paul VI. Another 24.1% (307) were edited in some way before their inclusion. A further 16.2% (206) were centonised with other prayers—effectively combining parts of multiple prayers together into a new oration. Fully 52.6% (669) of the prayers in the traditional Roman Rite have been excised from the modern liturgy, memory-holed by the *Consilium ad exsequendam*" (Matthew Hazell, "'All the Elements of the Roman Rite'? Mythbusting, Part II," *New Liturgical Movement*, October 1, 2021, www.newliturgicalmovement.org/2021/10/all-elements-of-roman-rite-mythbusting.html). On the principles that guided this massive revision of the Missal's orations, see Lauren Pristas, "Theological Principles of the Roman Missal (1970)," in *The Thomist* 67 (2003): 157–95.

of communion in the hand.[29] The *Novus Ordo* does not hesitate
to contradict the conciliar constitution openly on several points.
This is particularly obvious with regard to the use of the Latin
language and Gregorian chant, which has become optional and,
de facto, abandoned.[30]

The same is true as regards the amount of freedom left to the
celebrant. Although the Second Vatican Council emphasized
that "regulation of the sacred liturgy depends solely on the
authority of the Church" and "therefore no other person, even

---

[29] On the instruction *Memoriale Domini* of May 29, 1969 introducing the lat-
ter practice, see *Bref examen critique de la communion dans la main* (Versailles:
Contretemps, 2021); Federico Bortoli, *La distribution de la communion dans la
main. Études historiques, canoniques et pastorales* (Perpignan: Artège, 2019); Peter
Kwasniewski, *Holy Bread of Eternal Life: Restoring Eucharistic Reverence in an
Age of Impiety* (Manchester, NH: Sophia Institute Press, 2020).

[30] *SC* 36 provided that "particular law remaining in force, the use of the Latin
language is to be preserved in the Latin rites." *SC* 116 stated that "the Church
acknowledges Gregorian chant as specially suited to the Roman liturgy: therefore, other things being equal, it should be given chief place [*principem locum*] in
liturgical services." But in his General Audience of November 26, 1969, Paul VI,
in presenting the new rite of the Mass, would explain that "no longer Latin, but
the spoken language will be the principal language of the Mass. The introduction
of the vernacular will certainly be a great sacrifice for those who know the beauty,
the power and the expressive sacrality of Latin. We are parting with the speech
of the Christian centuries; we are becoming like profane intruders in the literary
preserve of sacred utterance. We will lose a great part of that stupendous and
incomparable artistic and spiritual thing, the Gregorian chant. We have reason
indeed for regret, reason almost for bewilderment." For commentary, see Peter
Kwasniewski, *The Once and Future Roman Rite: Returning to the Traditional Latin
Liturgy after Seventy Years of Exile* (Gastonia, NC: TAN Books, 2022), 109–43.

if he be a priest, may add, remove, or change anything in the liturgy on his own authority" (*SC* 22), the new Missal—which does not precisely regulate the gestures, attitudes, or often even the words of the priest—rather constantly invites him to be creative, by means of purely indicative or optional rubrics such as: *Sacerdos dicit sic vel simili modo* . . . or: *Hic sacerdos potest dicere,* or again: *pro opportunitate* . . . , *si placet* . . . , *expedit ut* . . . , *vel* . . . *vel* . . . *vel* . . . Many studies have shown that this is one of the fundamental marks of the new liturgy: it is *by its very nature* multiform and evolving.[31] Such variations according to

---

[31] Already in 1969, Fr. Roguet, a member of the *Consilium*, emphasized this characteristic feature of the new rite: "It must be said that from now on the liturgy changes, I mean that it is *mobile*. In the past, in the Latin Church, everyone had to observe exactly the same rules in all circumstances. An abbey or cathedral church, a suburb or village parish, a nun's chapel, a mission station: all had to practice the same ceremonial. The 'sung Mass' constituted a solid block; so did the 'low Mass.' Today this is no longer the case. *By obeying the new rules,* one can sing this or that part of the Mass *as one pleases.* If one does not sing, such a processional chant will simply be omitted, except for its antiphon. The priest remains *free* in his choice of the four Eucharistic Prayers; he may take from the Lectionary, *at will,* a reading that seems important to him, which would otherwise have been obstructed by the occurrence of a feast; he *may* say another oration than that of the day; if he celebrates for a small group, he *may* make certain simplifications. . . . If the ordinary of the Mass remains a more or less [!] stable framework, it is not certain that, in certain countries at least, new Eucharistic Prayers will not be created" (Aimon-Marie Roguet, O.P., *Table ouverte. La messe d'aujourd'hui* [Paris: Desclée, 1969]). The author logically concludes that hand missals for the faithful have become useless: "With the freedom the present liturgy allows, we cannot always know in advance which prayers, which readings, which Eucharistic Prayer the priest is

the will of the celebrant are therefore in no way "abuses": they are *prescribed* by what must be called, despite the oxymoron, a "protean rite." Whether a rite without binding forms[32] or well-defined practices is still a rite is not for us to examine here.[33] Suffice it to note that the rite of Paul VI would certainly

going to choose: by the time we find them in our book, they are finished, or already very advanced, without our having heard anything!" We might note a "curiosity" in the recent publication of a congregational hand missal for the new rite, but in the "old style": Thomas Diradourian, ed., *Laudate. Missel grégorien des fidèles* (Perpignan: Artège, 2021).

[32] Historian Roberto de Mattei indicates that the classical definition of "rite" goes back to Servius: "*Mos institutus religiosis cæremoniis consecratus*" (Servius, *Aen.*, 12, 836 a). A rite is therefore not the sacred action itself, but the *norm* which guides the unfolding of this action (cf. Roberto de Mattei, "Reflections on the Liturgical Reform," in *Looking Again at the Question of the Liturgy with Cardinal Ratzinger*, ed. Alcuin Reid [Farnborough, UK: St. Michael's Abbey Press, 2003], 135). The liturgist Klaus Gamber defines "rite" as "mandatory forms of the liturgical cult that, in the final analysis, originated with Christ, and then, based on shared traditions, developed independently, and were later officially sanctioned by the Church hierarchy" (*The Reform of the Roman Liturgy: Its Problems and Background*, trans. Klaus D. Grimm [Fort Collins, CO: Roman Catholic Books, n.d.], 27).

[33] Cardinal Ratzinger had raised the question as follows: "Today we might ask: *Is there a Latin Rite at all any more?* Certainly there is no awareness of it.... There was a loss of the awareness of 'rite,' that is, that there is a prescribed liturgical form and that liturgy can only be liturgy to the extent that it is beyond the manipulation of those who celebrate it" ("Change and Permanence in Liturgy: Questions to Joseph Ratzinger," in *Collected Works*, vol. 11: *Theology of the Liturgy*, ed. Michael J. Miller [San Francisco: Ignatius Press, 2014], 523). On the new relation to "norms" in the reformed liturgy, cf. Hélène Bricout (ed.), *Du bon usage des normes en liturgie. Approche théologique et spirituelle après Vatican II* (Paris: Cerf, 2019).

never have received the assent of the majority of the Council Fathers. This observation is not a retrospective judgment, made fifty years after the reform. It was immediate and obvious, as can be seen from the following lines, written "on the spot" in 1969, as a conclusion to the *Short Critical Study of the Novus Ordo Missae* endorsed by Cardinals Ottaviani and Bacci (the so-called "Ottaviani Intervention"):

> It is well-known how Vatican II is now being repudiated by the very men who once gloried in being its leaders. While the pope declared at the Council's end that it had changed nothing, these men came away determined to "explode" the Council's teachings in the process of actually applying it. Unfortunately the Holy See, with inexplicable haste, approved and even seemingly encouraged through [the] *Consilium* an ever-increasing infidelity to the Council. This infidelity went from changes in mere form (Latin, Gregorian Chant, suppression of ancient rites, etc.) all the way to the changes in substance which the *Novus Ordo* sanctions.[34]

Indeed, not only was the new rite not "the Mass of Vatican II," but it was a break with everything that had preceded it.

---

[34] Cardinals Alfredo Ottaviani and Antonio Bacci, *Short Critical Study of the New Order of Mass (The Ottaviani Intervention)*, trans. Anthony Cekada (West Chester, OH: Philothea Press, 2010), 73.

The Rite of Paul VI Is Not in Homogeneous Continuity with the Previous Rite

Although the Second Vatican Council posited as a guiding principle of liturgical reform "that any new forms adopted should in some way grow organically from forms already existing" (*SC* 23), the new Missal establishes an entirely new rite, a *ritus modernus* (to use the expression of the eminent liturgist Klaus Gamber[35]), which far from being in homogeneous continuity with the previous rite—the *ritus romanus*—has only a distant kinship with it.[36] This fact of non-continuity is granted by many liturgists, whether they praise it or deplore it.

Thus, Fr. Joseph Gélineau, a member of the *Consilium*[37] and a great supporter of the reform, could write:

Let those who like myself have known and celebrated a Latin and Gregorian High Mass remember it if they can. Let them compare it with the Mass that we now have. Not only the words, the melodies, and some of the gestures are different. In truth, it is a different liturgy of the Mass. This needs to be said in no uncertain terms:

---

[35] Gamber, *Reform of the Roman Liturgy*, 23.

[36] For a comprehensive demonstration of this claim, see Kwasniewski, *Once and Future Roman Rite*.

[37] The *Consilium ad exsequendam constitutionem de sacra liturgia*, instituted by Paul VI on January 25, 1964 with the motu proprio *Sacram Liturgiam*, was in charge of implementing the conciliar Constitution on the liturgy; its Secretary was Fr. Annibale Bugnini, C.M.

the Roman Rite as we knew it has ceased to exist. It has been destroyed.[38]

As if echoing Fr. Gélineau's words, Msgr. Gamber noted:

At this critical juncture, the traditional Roman rite, more than one thousand years old and until now the heart of the Church, was destroyed.... Obviously, the reformers wanted a completely new liturgy, a liturgy that differed from the traditional one in spirit as well as in form....[39]

There was no doubt that this was the very intention of the members of the *Consilium*. Two years before the promulgation of the new Missal, Fr. Annibale Bugnini himself had revealed the goal of the reform:

The liturgy is in the midst of a period of transition.... It is *not only a question of touching up* a work of art of great value, but sometimes it is necessary to give *new structures to entire rites*. It is indeed a question of a *fundamental restoration*, I would almost say of a *recasting* and, for certain points, of an *actual new creation*. Why this fundamental work? Because the image of the liturgy given by the Council is *completely different* from what it was before, that is, above all rubricist, formalist, centralizing. *Now*, the liturgy

---

[38] Joseph Gélineau, S.J., *Demain la liturgie. Essai sur l'évolution des assemblées chrétiennes* (Paris: Cerf, 1976), 10.

[39] Gamber, *Reform of the Roman Liturgy*, 99; 100.

expresses itself vigorously in its dogmatic, biblical, and pastoral aspects; it seeks to make itself intelligible in the word, in symbols, in gestures, in signs; it strives to *adapt itself* to the mentality, to the genius, to the aspirations, and to the demands of each people, in order to penetrate it intimately and to bring Christ there. *From a juridical point of view,* its fate is largely in the hands of the episcopal conferences, sometimes of the bishops, if not even of the *celebrating priests.* If the restored liturgy—which some disparagingly call the "new" liturgy—did not achieve *this goal,* the work of restoration would fail.[40]

"New structures," "recasting," "an actual new creation," "a completely different liturgy": the expressions used show unequivocally the intent to completely recast the liturgy. Such is the "goal" that the *Consilium* set for itself. This is a far cry from the prudent recommendation of *SC* 23 that "any new forms adopted should in some way grow organically from forms already existing." And while *SC* 22 emphasized that the regulation of the liturgy is reserved to the authority of the Church, such that "no other person, even if he be a priest, may add, remove, or change anything in the liturgy on his own authority," Fr. Bugnini asserts that liturgical reform is, even "juridically," in the hands of the celebrating priests.

Paul VI himself, on several occasions, insisted on the radical novelty of the rite he was instituting, and on the fact that his

---

[40] Annibale Bugnini, C.M., "Press Conference," January 4, 1967, translated into French in *DC,* 1967, col. 829, emphasis ours.

reform was not, unlike previous reforms, a simple "updating" of an immutable and handed-down rite:

> We ask you to turn your minds once more to the *liturgical innovation* of the *new rite* of the Mass. This *new rite* will be introduced into our celebration of the holy Sacrifice starting from Sunday next which is the first of Advent, November 30. A *new* rite of Mass: a change in a venerable tradition that has gone on for centuries. This is something that *affects our hereditary religious patrimony*, which seemed to enjoy the privilege of being untouchable and settled. It seemed to bring the prayer of our forefathers and our saints to our lips and to give us the comfort of feeling faithful to our spiritual past, which *we kept alive to pass it on to the generations ahead....* This *change* will affect the ceremonies of the Mass. We shall become aware, perhaps with some feeling of annoyance, that *the ceremonies at the altar are no longer being carried out with the same words and gestures* to which we were accustomed—perhaps so much accustomed that we no longer took any notice of them. This *change* also touches the faithful.... We must prepare for this *many-sided inconvenience*. It is the kind of upset caused by every *novelty* that *breaks in* on our habits.... This *novelty* is no small thing.[41]

---

41 Paul VI, Address at the General Audience of November 26, 1969 (an unofficial English translation is available here: www.ewtn.com/catholicism/library/changes-in-mass-for-greater-apostolate-8969, emphasis ours). In this same speech, Paul

And at the end of that same speech, in giving practical indications to priests, the Pontiff contrasted the "Roman Missal" with the "new rite": "Priests who celebrate in Latin . . . may, until November 28, 1971, use *either the Roman Missal or the new rite*. If they take the *Roman Missal* (etc.). . . . If they use the *new rite* (etc.)."[42]

Another authoritative voice is that of Joseph Ratzinger. It is well known that before becoming bishop of Rome, he was a theologian, an expert at the Council, that he was interested in liturgical questions from an early age, and that as Cardinal Prefect of the Congregation for the Doctrine of the Faith, he closely followed the Roman discussions concerning the juridical status of the old Missal.[43] And as a disciple of Gamber, Ratzinger himself insisted many times on the radical novelty of the rite

---

VI insists on "the greatest novelty: that of language" (see n30 above). One week earlier, the same pope, while underlining that with the new rite the essence of the Mass remains the same, did not hesitate to speak of a "surprising change," something "extraordinary," "such a surprising novelty." Never in the history of the Church have such expressions been used to qualify a liturgical reform—not even that of Holy Week under Pius XII.

[42] Paul VI, General Audience, November 26, 1969.

[43] We refer here to the commission of cardinals instituted by John Paul II in 1982, which met several times during the 1980s and finally concluded, apparently almost unanimously, that the 1962 Roman Missal had never been abrogated. Cf. Jean Madiran, *Histoire de la messe interdite*, vol. 2 (Versailles: Via Romana, 2009), 109–11. For details about this commission, see the write-up by Cardinal Dario Castillón-Hoyos, "Risposte del Cardinale Presidente della Pontificia Commissione 'Ecclesia Dei' a certi quesiti," www.clerus.org/clerus/dati/2008-10/24-20/ castrillon_rispost.html.

of Paul VI—a rite which, according to him, has the congenital defect of having been entirely *fabricated* by "experts."

In his *Memoirs*, the future Benedict XVI deplored, with regard to the liturgical reform, that "things went further than expected: the old building was *demolished*, and another was built, to be sure largely using materials from the previous one and even using the old building plans."[44] In a 1977 interview with the editors of the international Catholic magazine *Communio*, he stated: "Liturgy does not come about through regulation. One of the weaknesses of the postconciliar liturgical reform can doubtless be traced to the armchair strategy of academics, drawing up things on paper that, in fact, would presuppose years of organic growth."[45]

---

[44] Joseph Ratzinger, *Milestones: Memoirs 1927–1977*, trans. Erasmo Leiva-Merikakis (San Francisco: Ignatius Press, 1998), 148; trans. slightly modified.

[45] Ratzinger, "Change and Permanence," 521. The "armchair strategy" could extend even to bistro tables, as another eminent member of the *Consilium*, Louis Bouyer, recounted: "You'll have some idea of the deplorable conditions in which this hasty reform was expedited when I recount how the second Eucharistic prayer was cobbled together. Between the indiscriminately archeologizing fanatics who wanted to banish the *Sanctus* and the intercessions from the Eucharistic prayer by taking Hippolytus's Eucharist as is, and those others who couldn't have cared less about his alleged *Apostolic Tradition* and wanted a slapdash Mass, Dom Botte and I were commissioned to patch up its text with a view to inserting these elements, which are certainly quite ancient—by the next morning!... I cannot reread that improbable composition without recalling the Trastevere café terrace where we had to put the finishing touches to our assignment in order to show up with it at the Bronze Gate by the time our masters had set!" (*Memoirs*, trans. John Pepino [Kettering, OH: Angelico Press, 2015], 221–22).

In this regard, Joseph Ratzinger often emphasized how far removed the reform of Paul VI is from that of St. Pius V in its method of proceeding.

> The Council of Trent did not "make" a liturgy. Strictly speaking, there is no such thing, either, as the Missal of Pius V. The Missal which appeared in 1570 by order of Pius V differed only in tiny details from the first printed edition of the Roman Missal of about a hundred years earlier. . . . The new Missal was published as if it were a book put together by professors, not a phase in a continual growth process. *Such a thing has never happened before.* It is absolutely contrary to the laws of liturgical growth, and it has resulted in the nonsensical notion that Trent and Pius V had "produced" a Missal four hundred years ago.[46]

It is exactly this "nonsensical notion" that is found in the Letter accompanying *TC*, where Pope Francis invokes the alleged precedent of St. Pius V to justify his decision to make the reformed liturgical books the sole expression of the *lex orandi* of the Latin Church:

> I take the firm decision to abrogate all the norms, instructions, permissions and customs that precede the present motu proprio, and declare that the liturgical books promulgated by the saintly Pontiffs Paul VI and John Paul

---

[46] Ratzinger, "Change and Permanence," 523–24, emphasis ours.

II, in conformity with the decrees of Vatican Council II, constitute the unique expression of the *lex orandi* of the Roman Rite. I take comfort in this decision from the fact that, after the Council of Trent, St. Pius V also abrogated all the rites that could not claim a proven antiquity, establishing for the whole Latin Church a single *Missale Romanum*. For four centuries this *Missale Romanum*, promulgated by St. Pius V, was thus the principal expression[47] of the *lex orandi* of the Roman Rite, and functioned to maintain the unity of the Church.

Pope Francis seems to be saying to traditionalists, "What St. Pius V once did, I do myself." Yet, St. Pius V did the exact opposite of what Pope Francis claims to do in his motu proprio. Certainly, St. Pius V imposed a single Roman Missal, but this was not a *new* Missal like that of Paul VI, which Francis now claims to impose on the Latin Church; rather it was the ancient Roman Missal, *restored* according to the decrees of the Council of Trent, i.e., hardly altered at all from its medieval versions.[48]

---

[47] It is interesting to note that here the Holy Father did not dare write "unique."

[48] See Alcuin Reid, *The Organic Development of the Liturgy*, second ed. (San Francisco: Ignatius Press, 2005), 41: "The fundamental principle of this reform was indeed one of restoration. But it was not a restoration based on Protestant, iconoclast or antiquarian principles, nor was it a reform that sought to innovate. It was a restoration that sought to recover the beauty of the Roman Liturgy. The organism was pruned that it might flower again. Certainly, 'the standard of the commission was antiquity,' but by antiquity the commission understood the developed Roman Liturgy of the eleventh century: the missal of the Roman

It is for this very reason—namely, its antiquity—that this Missal has been such a factor of unity in the Church. For the unity of the Church is not only to be understood synchronically, but also diachronically.[49] In fact, the Roman Missal approved by St. Pius V contributed powerfully to both of those aspects. Through the precision of its rubrics, which left nothing to chance or improvisation but conferred on every gesture and posture of the ministers a hieratic quality marked by noble simplicity, by its doctrinal impeccability[50] and its very pure expression of the *lex credendi*, it favored the synchronic unity of the Church. Through its essentially traditional character, as a fruit of homogeneous development, it favored the diachronic unity of the Church. It contains prayers that are thousands of years old, prayers that have accompanied the entire history of

Curia spread by the mendicants. . . . Antiquity, then, as recognized and respected by the liturgical reform of St. Pius V, included what twentieth century liturgists deprecate as relatively late, and therefore corrupt, liturgical forms."

[49] "It is of the very essence of the Church that she should be aware of her unbroken continuity throughout the history of faith, expressed in an ever-present unity of prayer," remarked Ratzinger ("Change and Permanence," 525).

[50] See Council of Trent, Session 22, Doctrine on the Most Holy Sacrifice of the Mass, September 17, 1562, ch. 4: On the Canon of the Mass, in *Denz.-Hün.*, no. 1745: "Holy things must be treated in a holy way, and so, that this sacrifice might be worthily and reverently offered and received, the Catholic Church many centuries ago instituted the sacred canon. It is *so free from all error* that it contains nothing that does not savor strongly of holiness and piety and nothing that does not raise up to God the minds of those who offer. For it is made up of the words of the Lord himself, of apostolic traditions, and of devout instructions of the holy pontiffs" (emphasis added).

the Church and that still connect us today, as regards the oldest parts, to the first known testimonies of the liturgy in the West (third to fourth centuries).[51]

The *ritus modernus* of Paul VI is unable to fulfill this doubly unifying function of the Missal of St. Pius V. Its protean character prevents synchronic unity, since its creativity often leads, as Pope Francis himself recognizes in the accompanying Letter, "to almost unbearable distortions"; its novel character prevents diachronic unity, since it differs, both in its spirit and in its external forms, from the Roman Rite as celebrated until then.

Finally, the reform of Paul VI differs profoundly from that of Pius V, in that the Dominican pope, in promulgating his

---

[51] "Essentially the Missal of Pius V is the Gregorian Sacramentary; that again is formed from the Gelasian book, which depends upon the Leonine collection. We find the prayers of our Canon in the treatise *de Sacramentis* and allusions to it in the IVth century. So our Mass goes back, without essential change, to the age when it first developed out of the oldest Liturgy of all. It is still redolent of that Liturgy, of the days when Caesar ruled the world and thought he could stamp out the faith of Christ, when our Fathers met together before dawn and sang a hymn to Christ as to God... [T]here is not in Christendom another rite so venerable as ours" (Adrian Fortescue, *The Mass: A Study of the Roman Liturgy* [London: Longmans, Green & Co., 1913], 213, quoted in Alcuin Reid, *Organic Development*). Cf. Michael Fiedrowicz, *The Traditional Mass. History, Form, and Theology of the Classical Roman Rite* (Brooklyn, NY: Angelico Press, 2020), especially Part I: History. Paul VI himself acknowledged this in the first paragraph of his Apostolic Constitution *Missale Romanum* promulgating the new rite of the Mass, in which, speaking of the Missal promulgated by St. Pius V, he stated: "Innumerable holy men have abundantly nourished their piety towards God by its readings from Sacred Scripture or by its prayers, *whose general arrangement goes back, in essence, to St. Gregory the Great*" (April 3, 1969, in *AAS* 61:217).

Missal, respected all the rites—of which there were many[52]—that could claim an antiquity of over two hundred years.[53] On this point again, Joseph Ratzinger had several times underlined the fundamental difference between the two reforms:

> In this regard, it should be remembered that the way in which the new Missal was introduced departs from the juridical practice of the past, as observed, for example, by St. Pius V in his reform of the Missal, which explicitly provided that "*nequaquam auferimus*" in relation to any "*consuetudo*" ["in no way whatsoever do we take away any custom"] observed for over 200 years. Therefore, for instance, in Cologne and Trier, until the eighteenth century, and in Milan until Vatican II, another type remained in use, as was the case also in the Dominican order; and it would be easy to find other examples. Thus, the Missal of Pius V was not

---

[52] Although only a few survived down to the pontificate of Paul VI (the rites of certain religious orders, the Mozarabic, Ambrosian, and Lyons rites, etc.), this was for accidental reasons that had to do with the advent of the printing press. The Roman Missal approved by St. Pius V was the most printed and the most widely distributed, such that many dioceses would give up their own rite and adopt the former rather than having to print a local missal at great expense.

[53] Such that—as more than one commentator has mischievously remarked—"the modern rite of Paul VI, under the Grand Inquisitor, would have been elegantly crossed out, without any hope, not even a remote one, of being able to triumph as the sole rite of all Christendom" (Cristiana de Magistris, "An Act of Weakness," in *From Benedict's Peace to Francis's War: Catholics Respond to the Motu Proprio* Traditionis Custodes *on the Latin Mass*, ed. Peter A. Kwasniewski [Brooklyn, NY: Angelico Press, 2021], 182).

a new Missal, but a particular form of the Roman Missal which was in use in the city of Rome, very little altered according to the sources, or in other words, nothing more than the circle of growth of the old trunk, developed in a linear way, following a process that goes back to the time of Hippolytus. For this reason I find it historically false and theologically fatal to speak of the "Tridentine Mass" or the " Missal of Pius V." The problem of the new Missal lies, on the contrary, in its abandonment of a historical process that had always gone on, before and after St. Pius V, and in the creation of an entirely new book, albeit from ancient material, and whose publication was accompanied by a kind of ban on what had existed before, a ban, moreover, never seen in juridical and liturgical history. I can say with confidence, based on my knowledge of the conciliar debates and from rereading the speeches of the Council Fathers delivered at the time, that this does not correspond to the intentions of the Second Vatican Council.[54]

In the light of this, the question of the legitimacy of the reform undertaken by Paul VI inevitably arises. Did the pope have the

---

[54] Joseph Ratzinger, Letter to Professor Wolfgang Waldstein, Regensburg, December 14, 1976, original German text in "Zum motu proprio *Summorum Pontificum*," *Una Voce Korrespondenz* 38/3 (2008), 201–14; Italian translation in Antonio Sánchez Gil, "Gli innovativi profili canonici del motu proprio *Summorum Pontificum* sull'uso della Liturgia romana anteriore alla riforma del 1970," in *Ius Ecclesiæ* XIX (2007), 695–96.

right to change the centuries-old Roman Rite? To fabricate a new liturgical rite from scratch and ban the old one? And does the present pope have the right to decide that the rite of Paul VI is the sole expression of the *lex orandi*?

The Question of the Legitimacy of the *Novus Ordo Missae*

Article 3 §1 of *TC* enjoins diocesan bishops to ensure that groups requesting to celebrate according to the 1962 Missal "do not deny the validity *and the legitimacy* of the liturgical reform." This requirement regarding legitimacy was already part of the Circular Letter of the Sacred Congregation for Divine Worship *Quattuor Abhinc Annos* of October 3, 1984, giving diocesan bishops the faculty to allow celebrations according to the old Missal.[55] However, it was not included in the Protocol Agreement of May 5, 1988 between Cardinal Ratzinger and Archbishop Lefebvre. No. 4 of that Protocol only mentioned validity:[56] "Moreover, we declare that we recognize the validity of the Sacrifice of the Mass and the Sacraments celebrated with the intention of doing

---

[55] "That it be made publicly clear beyond all ambiguity that such priests and their respective faithful in no way share the positions (*nullam partem habere cum iis*) of those who call in question the legitimacy and doctrinal exactitude of the Roman Missal promulgated by Pope Paul VI in 1970" (French text in *DC* 1984, p. 1125).

[56] Archbishop Lefebvre's position was always to recognize the validity of the New Mass with regard to the essence of the sacrament and thus as to its strictly sacramental effectiveness. See "Mgr Lefebvre et le Saint-Office," *Itinéraires* 233 (1979): 146.

what the Church does, and according to the rites indicated in the typical editions of the Roman Missal and the Rituals of the Sacraments promulgated by Popes Paul VI and John Paul II."[57] Now, that Protocol Agreement remains normative for institutes that were erected by the Holy See in accordance with the motu proprio *Ecclesia Dei* of July 2, 1988, which expressly refers to it. The purpose was "facilitating full ecclesial communion of priests, seminarians, religious communities or individuals until now linked in various ways to the Fraternity founded by Archbishop Lefebvre, who may wish to remain united to the Successor of Peter in the Catholic Church, while preserving their spiritual and liturgical traditions, in the light of the Protocol signed on May 5 last by Cardinal Ratzinger and Archbishop Lefebvre."[58] The Holy See had explicitly committed to this, assuring them that "all measures will be taken to guarantee their [existing] identity, in full communion with the Catholic Church."[59] By virtue of the legal

---

[57] *Protocol Agreement between the Holy See and Archbishop Lefebvre*, Doctrinal Declaration, no. 4, in *DC* 1988, p. 734. Furthermore, no. 3 affirmed: "With regard to certain points taught by the Second Vatican Council or concerning subsequent reforms of the liturgy and law, which seem to us to be difficult to reconcile with Tradition, we commit ourselves to a positive attitude of study and communication with the Apostolic See, avoiding all polemics." (English version available here: https://fsspx.org/en/protocol-agreement-may-5-1988.)

[58] Apostolic Letter *Ecclesia Dei Adflicta* of the Supreme Pontiff John Paul II given *motu proprio*, July 2, 1988, no. 6a, in *DC* 1988, p. 789 (English version available on the Vatican website).

[59] Informatory Note of June 16, 1988: *L'Osservatore Romano*, English ed., June 27, 1988, pp. 1–2.

maxim "*pacta sunt servanda*," no more should be required of these institutes than was required at the time of their erection.

What is meant when one refers to the "legitimacy" of the liturgical reform?[60] As etymology would suggest, that which is legitimate (or licit) is that which has been legally established. This may be understood in several ways. A juridical act (whether administrative, legislative, or judicial) is legitimate if it has been posited in accordance with the formalities and requirements of the law (cf. can. 124). However, more fundamentally, such an act must exhibit those constitutive elements that are essential to it. Thus, a normative juridical act can be issued by the relevant authority only within its own area of jurisdiction, in order to regulate those things which fall under its *dominium*. Even if the legal formalities had been complied with, a normative statement uttered by someone who does not have *dominium* over the reality he claims to regulate, is not a juridical norm, but, at most, a proposed norm. Consequently, a normative act is legitimate only if it conforms to the nature of things, because such nature does not fall under the *dominium* of men. No human authority can establish an *order* that goes against this reality. A "juridical norm" that would be contrary to the nature of things would not be rational, and, in fact, it would not be a norm at all. Such a norm does not introduce an order; it introduces a disorder. It

---

[60] This refers to the liturgical reform *in fieri*. An entirely different question would be that of the legitimacy of the reform *in facto esse*, i.e., of the legitimacy of the celebration or participation in the reformed rite.

is not just, but rather *vis* and *iniuria*.[61] Let us attempt to apply these principles to the liturgical reform of Paul VI.

Considering solely the new Missal, no one disputes that it was promulgated by the legitimate authority according to the legal forms, namely by Pope Paul VI in the Apostolic Constitution *Missale Romanum* of April 3, 1969.

Nor is it because it certainly went beyond the intentions of the Second Vatican Council that the liturgical reform of Paul VI might be considered illegitimate. The pope "possesses in the Church, by virtue of his office, ordinary, supreme, plenary, immediate and universal power, which he can always exercise freely" (can. 331). Paul VI alone, therefore, had no less authority than the Second Vatican Ecumenical Council (with Paul VI and never without him, *cum Petro et sub Petro*), and he was no more bound by the conciliar decisions than he was by his own decisions or those of his predecessors. From this purely canonical point of view, the question of whether the reform carried out by Paul VI is indeed what was requested by Vatican II, is irrelevant.

The real question is, rather, that of the limits of the Supreme Pontiff's authority in liturgical matters. In modern times, in the West, popes have appropriated the right to legislate in an

---

[61] That is, violence or force, and injury. Cf. St. Thomas, *Sum. theol.*, Ia-IIae, q. 93, a. 3, ad 2: "Human law has the nature of law in so far as it partakes of right reason; and it is clear that, in this respect, it is derived from the eternal law. But in so far as it deviates from reason, it is called an unjust law, and has the nature not of law but of violence."

ever more detailed and extensive manner in liturgical matters. This phenomenon increased even more in the twentieth century, under the combined effect of a juridical positivism that was very prevalent (even in the Church),[62] and of an ecclesiology that tended to absolutize the power of the pope.[63] So much so that, as noted by Joseph Ratzinger, "after the Second Vatican Council, the impression arose that the pope really could do anything in liturgical matters, especially if he were acting on the mandate of an ecumenical council."[64] It is true that the power of the bishop of Rome is "supreme," in the sense that it is not subordinate to any human power, and "plenary," in the sense that it possesses in its fullness all the power that Christ has given to his Church

---

[62] Cf. Carlos José Errázuriz, "Positivismo jurídico," in *DGDC*, vol. VI, 276–80, especially 278–80: "Positivismo jurídico y derecho canónico."

[63] Yves Congar denounced this ecclesiological drift more than once: "The hierarchy was completely centered on the Roman pontiff, in a perspective of true spiritual monarchy. Not all classical manuals were as brutally frank as Domenico Palmieri, S.J., who chose to call his work *Tractatus de Romano Pontifice cum Prolegomenis de Ecclesia* (Rome, 1877; 2nd edition, Prato, 1891; 3rd edition, 1902). But . . . the Church appeared as a sort of inference or outgrowth of its Roman head" (Yves Congar, O.P., *Le concile de Vatican II. Son Église, Peuple de Dieu et Corps du Christ* [Paris: Beauchesne, 1984], 14–15). On the eve of the Second Vatican Council (November 8, 1961, in a communication to the Week of Catholic Intellectuals), he would state: "I could draw out of my files a good dozen texts, up to the last few years, stating principles similar to this: As there is only one faith, as there is only one See of Peter, so there must be one and the same discipline following the traditions and customs of the Roman Church" (*Sainte Église. Études et approches ecclésiologiques* [Paris: Cerf, 1963], 117).

[64] *Spirit of the Liturgy*, in Ratzinger, *Collected Works*, 11:102.

to teach, sanctify, and govern. But this power is not absolute and limitless, as if the pope's thought or will were law. It is at the service of the Church's holy and living Tradition, which it must always preserve and pass down. This is especially true in relation to the liturgy, which is one of the constitutive elements of that Tradition. Cardinal Ratzinger once explained this using the striking image of a gardener in his garden, as opposed to a technician who makes machines:

> The pope is not an absolute monarch whose will is law; rather, he is the guardian of the authentic tradition and, thereby, the premier guarantor of obedience. He cannot do as he likes, and he is thereby able to oppose those people who, for their part, want to do whatever comes into their head. His rule is not that of arbitrary power, but that of obedience in faith. That is why, with respect to the liturgy, he has the task of a gardener, not that of a technician who builds new machines and throws the old ones on the junk pile.[65]

---

[65] Foreword to Alcuin Reid's *The Organic Development of the Liturgy*, in Ratzinger, *Collected Works*, 11:591. This is a constant in Ratzinger's thought: "In fact the First Vatican Council had in no way defined the pope as an absolute monarch. On the contrary, it presented him as the guarantor of obedience to the revealed Word. The pope's authority is bound to the Tradition of faith, and that also applies to the liturgy. It is not 'manufactured' by the authorities. Even the pope can only be a humble servant of its lawful development and abiding integrity and identity. . . . The authority of the pope is not unlimited; it is at the service of Sacred Tradition" (*Spirit of the Liturgy*, IV.1, in *Collected Works*, 11:102–3).

The same is summarized in the *Catechism of the Catholic Church*, n. 1125: "Even the supreme authority in the Church may not change the liturgy arbitrarily, but only in the obedience of faith and with religious respect for the mystery of the liturgy."

Given the above, one understands that a pontifical liturgical law which does not respect the very nature of the liturgy would not be a law, a *regula iuris*, but rather a *corruptela iuris*, a corruption of the law, even if it were guaranteed by all juridical forms. It would lack that fundamental character of any law which is rationality. Since the act of law-making is an act of reason, it is itself conditioned, "normed," by the nature of things. Obviously, when the norm has all the external appearances of legitimacy, it is up to the one who denies its rationality to provide proof of this lack.[66]

There can, however, be inappropriate, questionable, defective liturgical norms[67] without being necessarily irrational nor,

---

[66] Eduardo Baura reminds us, however, that "in the event of evident irrationality, disobedience to the norm would be licit. This is precisely the justification for the non-application of the law in a particular case on the grounds of *epikeia*, and also sometimes the basis for the introduction of a custom *contra legem*" (*Parte generale del diritto canonico* [Rome: EDUSC, 2013], 140). Strictly speaking, one should not speak of "disobedience" in such a case, because the norm simply does not oblige and therefore there is no matter for obedience.

[67] In matters of liturgical discipline, the Magisterium has more than once underlined the possibility of deficiencies, within the limits set by the Catholic doctrine of divine assistance to the universal laws of the Church. Thus, according to Pius XII, "There are found in the liturgy unchangeable elements, a sacred content which transcends time, but also elements which are variable and transitory, and

consequently, illegitimate. A Catholic may, for example, find the reform of Holy Week under Pius XII, or the reform of the Code of Rubrics under John XXIII, questionable, unpastoral or inappropriate. Such norms, however, do not for this reason cease to be legitimate and obligatory, and in fact, their application did not meet with any resistance at the time, including in the most conservative circles, even though they might have been sometimes criticized.[68]

However, a norm that is completely inadequate to the reality which it claims to order, lacks legitimacy. And we consider it contrary to the very nature of a liturgical rite for it to be fabricated or manufactured. This is what Msgr. Gamber maintained:

> If we assume that the liturgical rite evolved on the basis of shared traditions—and nobody who has at least some

---

sometimes even imperfect" (Allocution to the Assisi Liturgical Congress, September 22, 1956, English version published as a Supplement to *Worship* [1957], 223–36). And the Second Vatican Council itself emphasized that there may be elements in the liturgy that need to be reformed if they "have suffered from the intrusion of anything out of harmony with the inner nature of the liturgy or have become unsuited to it" (*SC* 21).

[68] Regarding the reform of Pius XII, one may refer to the severe criticisms of Msgr. Léon Gromier (1879–1965), canon of the Vatican Basilica: "Simples réflexions sur des choses restaurées," in *Opus Dei* (1961), no. 5, 248–54, and "La Semaine Sainte restaurée," in *Opus Dei* (1962), no. 2, 76–90 (English trans. available here: https://civitas-dei.eu/gromier.htm). On the stakes of this reform: Patrick Prétot, O.S.B., "La réforme de la semaine sainte sous Pie XII (1951–1955). Enjeux d'un premier pas vers la réforme liturgique de Vatican II ," in *Questions liturgiques* 93 (2012): 196–217.

knowledge of liturgical history will dispute this—then it cannot be developed anew in its entirety. . . . Every liturgical rite constitutes an organically developed, homogeneous unit. To change any of its essential elements is synonymous with the destruction of the rite in its entirety. . . . The assertion, which continues to be made, that the inclusion of some parts of the traditional Missal into the new one means a continuation of the Roman rite, is unsupportable. . . . The countless innovations introduced as part of liturgical reform have left hardly any of the traditional liturgical forms intact.[69]

---

[69] Gamber, *Reform of the Roman Liturgy*, 27, 30-31, 34, 39. The latter remark is enough to rebut Pope Francis's statement in the Accompanying Letter, according to which "whoever wishes to celebrate with devotion according to earlier forms of the liturgy can find in the reformed Roman Missal according to Vatican Council II all the elements of the Roman Rite, in particular the Roman Canon which constitutes one of its more distinctive elements." Is there any need to recall, moreover, that even the Roman Canon—which in the reform became a "Eucharistic Prayer" among several others—did not remain intact in the *editio typica* of the Missal of Paul VI? See Roger-Thomas Calmel, O.P., "Réparation publique au canon romain outragé," in *Itinéraires* 206 (Sept.-Oct. 1976): 101–81. Cardinal Alfons Stickler observed that the disappearance of the words "*mysterium fidei*" from the words of consecration could be seen as a symbol of the desacralization, and thus the humanization, of the central core of the Mass (see "Recollections of a Vatican II Peritus," *New Liturgical Movement*, June 29, 2022, www.newliturgicalmovement.org/2022/06/recollections-of-vatican-ii-peritus-by.html). Let us recall that those very words already appear in the *Gelasian Sacramentary*, the oldest of the Roman Church. St. Thomas Aquinas states that they come from the Apostolic Tradition (*Sum. theol.*, IIIa, q. 78, a. 3, ad 9). For detailed commentary, see Kwasniewski, *Once and Future Roman Rite*, 263–77.

Thus, regardless of the consideration of its serious intrinsic ritual deficiencies, which make it an unsatisfactory expression of the *lex credendi*,[70] the mere fact that the *Novus Ordo Missæ* is a new and fabricated rite is sufficient for the canonist to question its legitimacy.

That being said, even if one were to admit (for the sake of argument) that a new authentic rite could be created from scratch by the will of a pope, such a new rite could only ever be optional, and could not simply replace a pre-existing rite.

The Impossible Abrogation of the Traditional Roman Missal

The question of whether a pope can legitimately prohibit a liturgical rite is not new in theology. Francisco Suárez, S.J. († 1617), for example, believed that a pope who would wish to change all rites

---

[70] Numerous studies have shown that the new rite of Mass poorly expresses essential truths of the faith, notably the Real Presence of Our Lord under the Eucharistic species, the sacrificial and propitiatory character of the Mass, and the distinction of nature (and not merely of degree) between the common priesthood and the ministerial priesthood. Suffice it to quote the works that appeared soon after the promulgation of the new Mass (some editions listed here are recent republications): Cardinals Ottaviani and Bacci, *Short Critical Study*; Louis Salleron, *La nouvelle messe*, 2nd ed. (Paris: NEL, 1976); Arnaldo Xavier da Silveira, *Two Timely Issues: The New Mass and the Possibility of a Heretical Pope*, trans. John Russell Spann and José Aloisio Schelini (Spring Grove, PA: The Foundation for a Christian Civilization, 2022); Michael Davies, *Pope Paul's New Mass* (Kansas City, MO: Angelus Press, 2009).

based on apostolic Tradition would be schismatic.[71] The question obviously resurfaced with the liturgical reform of Paul VI, which, as we have seen, involved a complete recasting of all the liturgical rites, particularly the rite of Mass. Was it possible for the new liturgy to simply replace the previous one?

As regards, at least, the Roman Missal, the question was *de facto* resolved in the negative. In *Summorum Pontificum*, Pope Benedict XVI stated: "It is therefore permitted to celebrate the Sacrifice of the Mass following the typical edition of the Roman Missal, which was promulgated by Blessed John XXIII in 1962 and *never abrogated*, as an extraordinary form of the Church's Liturgy."[72] For those who would see in this affirmation of non-abrogation of the old Missal a mere *obiter dictum* without any real impact, the pope himself, in the Letter accompanying the motu proprio, was careful to drive the point home: "As for the use of the 1962 Missal as a *Forma Extraordinaria* of the liturgy of the Mass, I would like to draw attention to the fact that this Missal was *never juridically abrogated* and, consequently, in principle, was *always permitted*."[73]

---

[71] Franciscus Suárez, *De Caritate*, disput. XII, sect. I, No. 2, in *Opera*, ed. Vivès, t. XII, p. 734: "*Et hoc secundo modo posset Papa esse schismaticus . . . si vellet omnes ecclesiasticas cæremonias apostolica traditione firmatas evertere.*"

[72] Benedict XVI, Apostolic Letter given *motu proprio Summorum Pontificum* on the Use of the Roman Liturgy Prior to the Reform of 1970, July 7, 2007, art. 1, in *AAS* 99 (2007): 779; emphasis ours.

[73] Benedict XVI, Letter to the Bishops on the Occasion of the Publication of the Apostolic Letter *motu proprio data Summorum Pontificum* on the Use of the

Indeed, the Apostolic Constitution *Missale Romanum* of Paul VI does not contain any explicit mention of the abrogation of the previous Missal (namely, that of the last *editio typica,* of 1962). Now, "in case of doubt"—and the plain fact that the Missal revised by St. Pius V continued to be used by many is sufficient to constitute such a doubt—"a revocation is not presumed" (cf. can. 21 *CIC*/83; can. 23 *CIC*/17).

Nonetheless, quite soon after the promulgation of the new Missal, various documents of uncertain authority coming from the Roman Curia or Episcopal Conferences tried to make the new rite mandatory.[74] Above all, Pope Paul VI himself declared,

---

Roman Liturgy Prior to the Reform of 1970, July 7, 2007, in *AAS* 99 (2007): 798, emphasis ours.

[74] In a Notification of June 14, 1971, the Congregation for Divine Worship had decided as follows: "From the day when the translations into the popular language in question are to be used in celebrations in the vernacular, only the new rite of Mass and of the Liturgy of the Hours may be used by those who continue to use the Latin language" (Sacred Congregation for Divine Worship, *Notificatio De Missali romano, liturgia horarum et calendario,* June 14, 1971, *AAS* 63 [1971]: 713). On November 14, 1974, the plenary assembly of the French episcopate had published a similar communiqué: "Some say that the use of the old *ordo missæ* known as that of Pius V may continue together with that of Paul VI. . . . The rules laid down on this point by Roman authority are clear and the will of the bishops of France is that they must be adhered to: the entire Missal promulgated by Pope Paul VI must replace the Missal of Saint Pius V. There can be no exception to this rule except for elderly or sick priests, in private celebrations without the assistance of the faithful, and with the express authorization of the bishop" (French Bishops' Conference, Communiqué de l'Assemblée plénière, November 14, 1974, in *DC* 71 [1974]: 1014). Responses along similar lines continued until the end of the 1990s.

in an address to the secret consistory of May 24, 1976, that "the use of the new *Ordo Missæ* is not at all left to the free will of the priests or the faithful (*usus novi Ordinis Missæ minime quidem sacerdotum vel christifidelium arbitrio permittitur*). . . . The new *Ordo* was promulgated to take the place of the old one after mature deliberation and for the carrying out of the norms bestowed by the Second Vatican Council (*Novus Ordo promulgatus est, ut in locum veteris substitueretur post maturam deliberationem, atque ad exsequendas normas quæ a Concilio Vaticano II impertitæ sunt*)." And he added: "It was not otherwise that our holy predecessor Pius V had made the reformed Missal obligatory under his authority."[75] Certainly, this was merely a papal speech, and cannot be considered as a juridical abrogation. Nevertheless, it leaves no doubt as to the intentions of the pope, who indeed intended to *prohibit* the old rite.

In an attempt to justify these surprising words of Paul VI, which—especially when read retrospectively in light of those of his successor Benedict XVI—look very much like an abuse of power, some authors have argued that the Missal of St. Pius V was not abrogated, but rather "obrogated" by the promulgation of the Missal of Paul VI.[76] The term "obrogation" refers to the

---

[75] Paul VI, *Allocutio in aula consistoriali palatii apostolici Vaticani*, May 24, 1976, *AAS* 68 (1976): 374; French trans. in *DC* 73 (1976): 558. It is clear that the strange argument made in the *TC* Accompanying Letter, according to which Francis proceeded in the same way as St. Pius V, is not new.

[76] For example, even recently: H. Donneaud, "Le pape François, garant de la doctrine liturgique de saint Pius V," 51, n22.

disappearance of a law by the substitution of a new law which is directly contrary to the previous one or which completely re-organizes the matter in question.[77] "*Lex posterior derogat priori.*" Canon 20 of the 1983 *Code of Canon Law* recalls this principle when it states: "A later law abrogates or derogates from an earlier law, if it expressly so states, or if it is directly contrary to that law, or if it integrally reorders the whole subject matter. . . ." Such, it is claimed, would be the case for the new Missal promulgated by Paul VI.

This kind of reasoning could perhaps be held (even though not without strong concessions to juridical positivism) in the case of a new *editio typica* of the *same* Missal that would obrogate the previous one. Thus, the revised Missals of Clement VIII, Urban VIII, Pius X, Benedict XV, Pius XII and John XXIII would each have obrogated the respective previous editions, since they are various successive states of the *same* rite. But this can in no way be said of the Missal of Paul VI, which creates a *ritus modernus*, substantially different from the *ritus romanus*. For there to be a complete reorganization of the matter, there must remain a matter, a subject of change. And to guarantee such permanence of the reorganized matter, it is certainly not enough to simply

---

[77] The Pio-Benedictine Code, then in force, used the term *obrogatio* to refer to all modes of revocation of the law. Canon 22 provided that "*Lex posterior, a competenti auctoritate lata, obrogat priori, si id expresse edicat, aut sit illi directe contraria, aut totam de integro ordinet legis prioris materiam....*" The new Code now uses the term only to refer the substitution of an administrative act by another that is contrary to it (cf. *CIC*/83 cann. 53 and 1739).

retain the name "*Missale Romanum*." To hold this would be to fall into the crudest nominalism.[78]

It is interesting to note that no priest was ever sanctioned under Benedict XV for using the previous Missal of St. Pius X, nor, under John XXIII, for continuing to use the Missal of Pius XII. With the liturgical reform of Paul VI, however, priests who would use an earlier edition of the Missal were suddenly the object of persecution, or at least were required to obtain special permission *ex indulto* in order to do so. It would never have occurred to a priest under John XXIII to request an indult to celebrate Mass with the Missal of Pius XII. There is a contradiction on the part of the reformers in maintaining that the new rite is substantially

---

[78] The opinion that the Roman Rite is simply the rite celebrated in Rome *hic et nunc* by the Roman Pontiff does not escape this reproach of nominalism. Like all authentic rites, the Roman Rite is an objective reality, the fruit of a homogeneous development, with permanent and easily identifiable liturgical characteristics. This curious and very positivistic conception of rite is voiced by Donneaud, who writes: "At every moment in history, the Roman Rite does not exist elsewhere than wherever the Eucharist is celebrated according to the concrete manner in which it is celebrated by the Holy Roman Church, and in particular its pontiff. . ."; or again: "The Roman Rite does not exist elsewhere, *in concreto*, than in the manner in which it is celebrated *in actu* by the Roman Church" ("Le pape François, garant de la doctrine liturgique de saint Pie V," 45 and 47). With such principles, one would have to say that the Roman Rite became, for a day, the Zaire rite, since the Holy Father celebrated a Mass according to this rite in St. Peter's itself, on December 1, 2021, first Sunday of Advent. Other such absurdities could be extrapolated. For a detailed defense of the claim that the Roman Rite has objectively stable defining characteristics that constitute it as a particular liturgy of apostolic derivation, see Kwasniewski, *Once and Future Roman Rite*, especially chs. 2 and 5.

identical to the previous one, while at the same time judging the celebration according to an earlier edition of the Missal to be abnormal, or even illicit without exceptional permission.

Moreover, Antonio Sánchez Gil has recently shown, quite convincingly, that the reasoning that claims the obrogation of one Missal by another reveals a normativistic and positivistic—"quasi-legalistic" (*sic*) logic. Such a logic could be understandable—even though probably erroneous in Church law[79]—in relation to the reform and replacement of a particular *legislative corpus*, but it is inadequate and incomprehensible if applied to the reform of a Missal or other liturgical book. The Missal or other liturgical books cannot be put on a par with regular laws which define ordinary legal regimes. If such were the case, their promulgation would necessarily imply, under canon 20, the complete abrogation of the preceding books, making their use unlawful except by special permission. The eminent professor draws attention to

> the danger of using a juridico-normative terminology
> and a logic proper to the world of law—with its technical
> and precisely defined vocabulary—in areas that are not

---

[79] Developing this vast question is beyond the scope of this work. Let us simply recall that even the *Codex iuris canonici* of 1917, which is clearly normativistic in spirit (as are modern civil codes), differs from these in the respect it shows for previous legislation. Canon 6 of the Pio-Benedictine *Code* had only a limited abrogatory force, and Canon 5 (albeit timidly) recognized custom as a source of law. The new *Code* was also intended to be firmly rooted in the *ius vetus* (as shown by the nine massive volumes of *Fontes*), and respectful of proper institutions of canon law.

properly juridical. In this sense, to speak of "promulgation" in reference to documents which, like a Missal or a ritual, are not laws in the formal sense, and do not contain norms that are properly juridical, could lead one to consider—as seems to have happened—that one can renovate the sacred liturgy and reform liturgical books in the same way as laws and juridical matters are reformed. But juridical matters follow their own logic and allow for a normative and legislative technique which, most probably, cannot be applied "as is" to matters which, like the sacred liturgy, follow a different logic.[80]

And he adds:

Certainly, the promulgation of a new Missal does not change its nature as a liturgical book, making it into a law, nor does it change its content (made up of rubrics and prayers: the rite to be followed in celebrating Holy Mass), as if this could transform "liturgical norms" and prayers into "juridical norms."[81] Although such an act

---

[80] Sánchez Gil, "Gli innovativi profili canonici del *motu proprio Summorum Pontificum*," 701.

[81] The author points out that the term "norm" is analogous. Juridical norms deal with relations of justice and a just social order; liturgical norms (rubrics) deal with the sacred rite to be performed in celebrations. Even if the latter have a juridical aspect, they cannot be considered as purely juridical norms. Legal norms must be observed for reasons of justice (including, but not limited to, legal justice). Liturgical norms are to be observed for reasons that go beyond justice—and certainly beyond legal justice—namely, the obedience of faith and religious

certainly has normative effects, since it determines the Missal to be used in the celebration of the Eucharist, it is very likely that it operates differently from the way in which the promulgation of a law operates.[82]

To clarify this, Sánchez Gil uses a helpful analogy: the promulgation of a new Catechism follows its own logic and certainly does not operate like the promulgation of a law. It would be absurd, for example, to argue that the promulgation of the *Catechism of the Catholic Church* "obrogated" and prohibited the *Catechism of the Council of Trent*. Similarly, the promulgation of a new edition of the Bible does not abrogate or prohibit a previous edition. In both cases, one speaks correctly of "promulgation,"[83] since such acts have a "normative" value. However, "promulgation" should be understood here in an analogous sense, because of the very particular nature of the "norms" being published, which follow a regime and a hermeneutic of their own. Bibles, catechisms, Missals, and the like are not juridical laws pure and simple.

---

reverence for the holy mysteries that are made present in the sacred rites. The author refers to *CCC*, no. 1125 and to Benedict XVI, Post-Synodal Apostolic Exhortation *Sacramentum Caritatis*, February 22, 2007, nos. 38 and 40, in *AAS* 99 (2007): 105–80.

[82] Sánchez Gil, "Gli innovativi profili canonici," 701.

[83] See, for the Catechism, John Paul II, Apostolic Constitution *Fidei Depositum*, October 11, 1992: "*probavimus . . . iubemus promulgationem . . . publici iuris facere*" (*AAS* 86 [1994]: 117); for the third edition of the *Nova Vulgata* of the Bible, John Paul II, Apostolic Constitution *Scripturarum Thesaurus*, April 25, 1979: "*editionem 'typicam' declaramus et promulgamus*" (*AAS* 71 [1979]: 559).

A Unique Expression of the Lex Orandi *of the Roman Rite?*

This is not the least of ironies: the liturgical reform of Paul VI, which was the exclusive work of liturgical and biblical experts who never ceased to denounce the "juridicism" and "rubricism" of the pre-conciliar Roman liturgy,[84] was carried out according to a juridico-normative, and even normativistic and positivistic, view. According to this view, a law is never more than the expression of the will of him who holds legislative power, who can create *ad libitum* a new law that abrogates the previous one. And the Missal itself, as well as the other liturgical books, are never more than sets of liturgical laws, expressions of the will of the supreme authority. It is difficult not to see this same logic at work in *TC*, when the latter states, in article 1, that "the liturgical books promulgated by Saint Paul VI and Saint John Paul II . . . are the unique expression of the *lex orandi* of the Roman Rite."

To contrast this positivistic view, it should be remembered that the pope himself is but the humble servant of the homogeneous development of the liturgy, of its integrity and of the permanence of its identity. A liturgical rite is more than a thousand-year-old custom: considered as a whole, it is a true Apostolic Tradition. For this reason, it is a juridically unavailable reality. It cannot be prohibited. "Such rites can die, if those who have used them in a particular era should disappear, or if the life-situation of those same people should change. The authority of the Church has the power to define and limit the use of such

---

[84] We have seen that Fr. Bugnini described it as "rubricist, formalist, centralizing" (see n39).

rites in different historical situations, but she never just purely and simply forbids them!"[85]

The fabrication of an entirely new rite has led, in the Latin Church, to an atypical situation of the coexistence of two rites for the same subjects. This situation is certainly unprecedented, as is the crisis that the Catholic Church has been going through for the past sixty years—one of the causes of which Cardinal Ratzinger saw precisely in the "disintegration of the liturgy."[86] Regardless, we have here a *de facto* situation which must be taken into account by the law, since it is reality that is normative. To regulate the use of the two rites, Pope Benedict XVI chose an innovative terminology, that of two "expressions"—"ordinary" and "extraordinary"—of the *lex orandi*. This allowed that Pontiff, while giving the *usus antiquior* a place, to support a hermeneutic of continuity between the two Missals, and to advocate for their mutual enrichment: "It is not appropriate to speak of these two versions of the Roman Missal as if they were 'two rites.' Rather, it is a matter of a twofold use of one and the same rite," he wrote in the Letter accompanying *Summorum Pontificum*. But while such a hermeneutic of continuity must be followed in principle regarding infallible magisterial teachings, the same is not necessarily true in relation to ritual forms, since these have their share

---

[85] Joseph Ratzinger, "Ten Years of the Motu Proprio *Ecclesia Dei*," a lecture given by Cardinal Ratzinger at the Ergife Palace Hotel, Rome, October 24, 1998, *Adoremus Bulletin*, December 31, 2007, https://adoremus.org/2007/12/ten-years-of-the-motu-proprio-quotecclesia-deiquot/.

[86] Ratzinger, *Milestones*, 148.

of contingency. That there is a continuity as to the essence of the sacrament is not in doubt, since in both rites, Holy Mass is indeed celebrated; but that there is a rupture as regards the rite is demonstrated by all the writings of the theologian Ratzinger. This rupture must be considered unfortunate, but it does not prevent "the continuity of the one Church-subject." By abandoning this questionable terminology of "two forms," *TC* provides serious arguments in favor of the acknowledgement of two *rites* in their own right.[†] Its mistake is to want to prohibit one of the two.

[†] [See *Addendum 1*, p. 99]

3

A Mishandling of Fundamental Principles of Canon Law

We have shown that the fundamental flaw in the new legislation lies in the irrational character of article 1, which states that the books reformed by Paul VI are the sole expression of the *lex orandi* of the Latin rite. However, the canonical anomalies do not, unfortunately, end there. We will highlight just a few: the failure to consider the proper law governing the ex-*Ecclesia Dei* institutes; the limitation of the prerogatives of diocesan bishops; the failure by the Congregation for Divine Worship to respect the principle of legality; finally, the absence of a *vacatio legis*.

Failure to Consider Proper Law

By simply stating, in article 6, that "institutes of consecrated life and societies of apostolic life, erected by the Pontifical

Commission *Ecclesia Dei*, fall under the competence of the Congregation for Institutes of Consecrated Life and Societies for Apostolic Life," the legislator does not seem to have taken into account what is implied by the existence in the Church of institutes whose identity includes a reasoned attachment to [previous] "charisms, traditions of spirituality and apostolate" and "previous liturgical and disciplinary forms of the Latin tradition."[87]

These institutes, whose constitutions have been definitively approved and which, according to the supreme legislator, "have today found proper stability of number and of life,"[88] have no existential foundation outside the framework of the traditional liturgy. The latter is, according to the very text of their constitutions, an essential element of their "project," of their "charism," of their "patrimony," in the sense of canon 578. Such patrimony is to be faithfully maintained by *all*, including the hierarchy[89] (*ab*

---

[87] John Paul II, *Ecclesia Dei*, no. 5.

[88] Francis, "Apostolic Letter issued *motu proprio* on the Pontifical Commission *Ecclesia Dei*," January 17, 2019.

[89] Cf. Louis-Marie de Blignières, F.S.V.F., "The Pope and the Law of Religious Institutes," *Sedes Sapientiae* Special English-language Issue, 2022, pp. 15–19 (an alternative translation also appeared at *Rorate Caeli* on January 28, 2022, https://rorate-caeli.blogspot.com/2022/01/authority-cannot-change-essential.html). Contrary to a widespread positivistic opinion, this study opportunely recalls, with quotations from classical authors, that "it is not in fact correct to affirm, without further qualification, that the pope may 'change the Constitutions approved by him.'. . . In the event of deviations or abuses, a Commissioner may be appointed, but he must always govern *according to the proper law* of the institute (Rule, Constitutions, Directory. . .). If circumstances are such that some of the

omnibus fideliter servanda sunt) (can. 578). For these institutes, the traditional liturgy and all traditional means and methods are more than just one thing among others within their patrimony. They are the determining cause of their foundation; they constitute their very *being*.

This is why these institutes have not simply received an indult which would allow them, in view of the particular and contingent circumstances of their foundation, to use the books prior to the liturgical reform of Paul VI. Rather, they enjoy *faculties*, i.e., a *right of their own*, a *special discipline*. The Protocol Agreement of May 5, 1988 between the Holy See and Archbishop Lefebvre, to which the motu proprio *Ecclesia Dei* refers, speaks, in effect, of a *particular law* granted to the institute as such, which is different from an indult (even if collective) to celebrate Mass for the benefit of priests or groups of faithful attached to the old rite.[90]

In the Church, the existence of an ordinary regime of law does not exclude—and in fact recognizes and presupposes—the

---

means previously employed are no longer feasible, or are no longer effective for obtaining the proper purpose of the institute, the hierarchy may, *for those reasons*, make changes to the Constitutions" (emphasis in original). The author notes that the hierarchy can also, in very serious and rare cases, suppress the Institute; yet it "cannot change its essential patrimony and its purpose."

[90] Protocol Agreement, Doctrinal Declaration, no. 5, in *DC* 1988, p. 734: "Finally, we promise to respect the common discipline of the Church and the ecclesiastical laws, especially those contained in the *Code of Canon Law* promulgated by Pope John Paul II, without prejudice to the *special discipline* granted to the Society by *particular law*" (emphasis ours). (English version available here: https://fsspx.org/en/protocol-agreement-may-5-1988.)

existence of special regimes of law. Special law must be considered by all as being in force, even if it only seems to concern a small number, because all must respect it. Therefore, even if restrictions or prohibitions on the use of previous liturgical books might be considered legitimate under the ordinary regime (which we in fact deny, since we have shown, at least as far as the traditional Roman Missal is concerned, that it cannot be abrogated), the institutes erected by the now defunct Pontifical Commission *Ecclesia Dei* would remain untouched by such measures.

In particular, the 1962 *Pontificale Romanum* was granted to these institutes as such. This concession is not for the direct benefit of the faithful, nor even only for the ordained individuals. It is granted to the clerical institute as such and for its benefit. For the ordaining bishops to receive the privilege of using the 1962 Pontifical, it is therefore sufficient that Major Superiors present their subjects to Holy Orders (together with the appropriate dimissorial letters). And the benefit of this practice falls to the institute, which has its subjects ordained in order to constitute its own clerics, for the service of its particular mission.

The *Responsa ad Dubia* of the CDW, which claim to prohibit or limit the use of the *Rituale Romanum* of 1952 (which is the last *editio typica*) and of the *Pontificale Romanum* completely ignore the existence of this proper law.

And this proper law regulates not only the life of the members within the houses of their institute, but also their apostolate outside, according to their proper charism. According to the *Code of Canon Law*, members of these institutes "must remain faithful to the discipline of the institute. If the need arises, bishops themselves are not to fail to insist on this obligation" (can. 678).[91]

The new legislation thus places on diocesan bishops the two-fold but contradictory onus of "working to return to a unitary form of celebration," while at the same time ensuring respect for the proper rights of institutes whose very identity is to celebrate according to the old rite. Clearly, it did not occur to the supreme legislator that there might be an inconsistency here.

[See *Addendum 2*, p. 100]

Diminishing the Prerogatives of Diocesan Bishops

Pope Francis has made "synodality"[92] and "healthy decentralization"[93] two major thrusts of his pontificate. In his first Apostolic

---

[91] Cf. can. 586 §1: "A true autonomy of life, especially of governance, is recognised for each institute. This autonomy means that each institute has its own discipline in the Church and can preserve whole and entire the patrimony described in can. 578."

[92] This term remains vague and ill-defined, as does the not unrelated term of ecclesial "communion." In a broad sense, it expresses "the participation of the faithful in the life of the Church, according to their own mode, with their own ministries, offices, and charisms" (Manoel Augusto Santos, "Sinodalidad," in *DGDC*, vol. VII, p. 341). Synodality is thus a broader concept than collegiality, since it involves not only the bishops but all the faithful and all structures. Cf. International Theological Commission, *Synodality in the Life and Mission of the Church*, March 2, 2018 (www.vatican.va/roman_curia/congregations/cfaith/cti_documents/rc_cti_20180302_sinodalita_en.html).

[93] The idea of a healthy Church decentralization is not new. It can already be found in the Preface of the 1983 *Code of Canon Law*, which ties it to the principle of subsidiarity: "On the basis of the same principle [of subsidiarity], the new *Code* entrusts either to particular laws or to executive power whatever is not necessary

---

Exhortation *Evangelii Gaudium*, which had a programmatic flavor, he wrote: "It is not advisable for the pope to take the place of local bishops in the discernment of every issue which arises in their territory. In this sense, I am conscious of the need to promote a sound 'decentralization.'"[94]

Yet it would be easy to show how—even under the guise of "synodality"—the present pontificate is characterized by a strong papal interventionism and a concentration of power in the pope's hands, unparalleled in the post-conciliar era.[95] *TC* is but a further illustration of this phenomenon.

---

for the unity of the discipline of the universal Church so that appropriate provision is made for a healthy 'decentralization' while avoiding the danger of division into or the establishment of national churches."

[94] Francis, Apostolic Exhortation *Evangelii Gaudium*, on the Proclamation of the Gospel in Today's World, November 24, 2013, in *AAS* 105 (2013): 1019–1137, no. 16.

[95] Suffice it to quote two examples. The first regards the erection of Institutes of Consecrated Life and Societies of Apostolic Life by diocesan bishops. Until 2020, canon 579 recognized the right of diocesan bishops, each in his own territory, to freely erect Institutes of Consecrated Life and Societies of Apostolic Life by formal decree, "*dummodo Sedes Apostolica consulta fuerit.*" With the motu proprio *Authenticum Charismatis* of November 1, 2020, Pope Francis modified the text of canon 579 as follows: "*Episcopi dioecesani, in suo quisque territorio, instituta vitæ consecratæ formali decreto erigere possunt, prævia licentia Sedis Apostolicæ scripto data*" (*L'Osservatore Romano*, November 4, 2020, p. 6). Bishops therefore now require the permission of the Holy See. The claims made in this *motu proprio* are illuminating. First of all, Francis reminds us that discernment on the authenticity of a charism and its ecclesiality belongs to the diocesan bishops. He then states that it is up to the Apostolic See to "accompany" them in this process of discernment. He concludes: "The new Institutes of Consecrated Life and the new Societies of Apostolic Life, *therefore*, must be officially recognized by the Apostolic See, which alone has

From its opening lines, the motu proprio states the intent to emphasize the role of the bishop as "moderator" of the liturgy in his own diocese:[96]

---

final judgment" (our emphasis). Continuing the same trend of centralization and demotion, the pope authorized a rescript on February 7, 2022, published on June 15, requiring diocesan bishops to receive written permission from the Dicastery for Institutes of Consecrated Life and Societies of Apostolic Life before they may erect a Public Association of the Faithful that seeks to become an institute or a society. This, too, effectively modified canon law, namely, cann. 312–313.

The second example has to do with the Synod of Bishops. It is well known how, since the beginning of his pontificate, Francis has made this advisory body to be in service to the Roman Pontiff as an efficient instrument for advancing his reforms—inserting, for example, that very personal reform regarding marriage nullity procedures in between the two synods on the family (motu proprio *Mitis Iudex Dominus Jesus*, August 15, 2015). Now, by the Apostolic Constitution *Episcopalis Communio* of September 15, 2018, the Synod of Bishops has been restructured. This measure considerably increases the role and competences of the General Secretariat of the Synod, which becomes the real driving force behind all synodal activity, by mandate and under the direct guidance of the pope, who is no longer content to passively receive the synodal work (as was the case until now), but actively promotes, coordinates, and directs it. It is therefore questionable whether the Synod of Bishops remains a consultative primatial body, or whether it is not rather an organ of primatial government; whether the Synod and the pope are "over against" one another or whether the former is in fact simply an emanation of the latter. In any event, the General Secretariat, which directs and stimulates the activity of the synod, appears to be a vicarious organ of government in the hands of the Holy Father. This position is all the more interesting if one remembers that the Synod is not part of the Roman Curia. See the interesting remarks of Bishop Juan Ignacio Arrieta, "Sinodalità e sinodo dei vescovi," in *Ius Ecclesiæ* 31/1 (2019): 275–88, especially 285.

[96] This is a truth stated by Vatican II. See *SC* 22: "*Sacræ liturgiæ moderatio ab Ecclesiæ auctoritate unice pendet: quæ quidem est apud Apostolicam Sedem et, ad normam iuris, apud Episcopum.*"

Guardians of the tradition, the bishops in communion with the bishop of Rome constitute the visible principle and foundation of the unity of their particular Churches. Under the guidance of the Holy Spirit, through the proclamation of the Gospel and by means of the celebration of the Eucharist, they govern the particular Churches entrusted to them.

In the accompanying Letter, Pope Francis emphasizes that he "desired to affirm that it is up to the bishop, as moderator, promoter, and guardian of the liturgical life of the Church of which he is the principle of unity, to regulate the liturgical celebrations." As a consequence, it is up to him to authorize, in his diocese, the use of the 1962 Roman Missal.

And indeed, article 2 of *TC* states:

It belongs to the diocesan bishop, as moderator, promoter, and guardian of the whole liturgical life of the particular Church entrusted to him, to regulate the liturgical celebrations of his Diocese. Therefore, it is his exclusive competence to authorize the use of the 1962 Roman Missal in his Diocese, according to the guidelines of the Apostolic See.

Considering the words "according to the directives of the Apostolic See," the detailed—if not fussy—provisions that follow show that the episcopal freedom thus proclaimed is in fact extremely limited and, above all, that it can be exercised only in one direction, namely, that of restricting the use of the traditional Missal until its complete and desired extinction. This impression is further reinforced when one reads the CDW's *Responsa ad Dubia*.

Thus, according to article 5 of *TC*, the diocesan bishop is to authorize priests who already celebrate according to the *usus antiquior* to continue to do so or not, on a case-by-case basis. In the case of restricting the exercise of acquired rights, the bishop's faculty is discretionary.[97] However, such is no longer the case when it comes to acknowledging new rights. Indeed, according to article 4, when dealing with new priests, i.e., priests ordained after the publication of the motu proprio,[98] the bishop must first

---

[97] Some bishops have thus been able to give free rein to their fantasy: Masses authorized only on certain days of the week, or on certain Sundays of the month, or only in certain places, or without the faithful, or during vacation time only. To get an idea of the creative imagination of bishops, one can consult the decree of the Cardinal-Archbishop of Chicago, Blase Cupich: Policy of the Archdiocese of Chicago for Implementing *Traditionis Custodes*, December 25, 2021, at the following address: www.chicagocatholic.com/chicagoland/-/article/2022/01/05/archdiocese-sets-policy-for-implementing-traditionis-custodes-.

[98] Neither *TC* nor the *Responsa* consider the case of a priest ordained before the publication of the motu proprio, who until then had celebrated Mass according to the missal of Paul VI, but who would now like to use that of John XXIII. Such a case falls within the scope of neither art. 5 (priests who were already celebrating according to the old) nor art. 4 (priests ordained after *TC*). This *lacuna legis*, created by the legislator himself, should be filled, taking into account can. 19, which refers to "general principles of law applied with canonical equity." Now, one of the *Regulæ iuris* states that "*Odia restringi, et favores convenit ampliari*" (VI° reg. 15). Obviously, a normativistic understanding, which considers that

consult the Apostolic See.[99] In addition, the *Responsa* interpret this article 4 in an extensive fashion, stating:

> This is not merely a consultative opinion, but a necessary authorization given to the diocesan bishop by the Congregation for Divine Worship and the Discipline of the Sacraments, which exercises the authority of the Holy See over matters within its competence (cf. *Traditionis Custodes*, n. 7). Only after receiving this permission will the diocesan bishop be able to authorize priests ordained after the publication of the *motu proprio* (July 16, 2021) to celebrate with the *Missale Romanum* of 1962. This rule is intended to assist the diocesan bishop in evaluating such a request: his discernment will be duly taken into account by the Congregation for Divine Worship and the Discipline of the Sacraments.[100]

---

there is no law outside of that which is established by the positive norm, would have a completely different interpretation here.

[99] "I presbiteri ordinati dopo la pubblicazione del presente motu proprio, che intendono celebrare con il *Missale Romanum* del 1962, devono inoltrare formale richiesta al Vescovo diocesano il quale prima di concedere l'autorizzazione consulterà la Sede Apostolica."

[100] We have seen that it was the same reasoning that justified the new wording of can. 579, instituting a system of prior authorization by the Holy See for the erection, by bishops, of Institutes of Consecrated Life of diocesan right. In both cases, we are assured that it is not a question of casting the slightest suspicion on the bishop's capacity for discernment (!), but rather of "helping" and "accompanying" him.

Now, in order to make an extensive interpretation such as this (which goes far beyond the meaning of the terms of the legal text, since it transforms a simple consultation into an authorization), the Dicastery, which does not enjoy legislative power, would have had to obtain either a prior delegation from the legislator, or an *a posteriori* approval given *in forma specifica*. This is not the case. It is therefore difficult to see how this interpretation could be binding.[101]

It is not only on the latter point that the *Responsa* go beyond the letter of the motu proprio, further restricting the power of bishops. We have seen that *TC* forbids the erection of new personal parishes and requires that, where there exist groups of faithful attached to the old rite, they not gather in parish churches. Given that in many dioceses there are no churches

---

[101] It is true that in support of its argument, the Dicastery quotes a Latin text, which it refers to as an "official reference text" (is this the future version to be published in the *Acta Apostolicae Sedis*?), which states in article 4: "*Presbyteri ordinati post has Litteras Apostolicas motu proprio datas promulgatas, celebrare volentes iuxta Missale Romanum anno 1962 editum, petitionem formalem Episcopo dioecesano mittere debent, qui, ante concessionem, a Sede Apostolica licentiam rogabit.*" Now, firstly, as of the date of the *Responsa*, this Latin version had not yet been published, and secondly, we have seen that the only authentic (reference) version is the *Italian* version found in *L'Osservatore Romano*, which in no way speaks of an authorization (*licentiam*), but only of a consultation: "[il vescovo] prima di concedere l'autorizzazione *consulterà* la Sede Apostolica" (our emphasis). The canonist remains confused before such incompetence on the part of a Dicastery of the Roman Curia. Unfortunately, these anomalies in the publication-promulgation of norms are anything but rare in the present pontificate. Cf. Geraldina Boni, *La recente attività normativa ecclesiale,* 70–71.

other than parish churches to accommodate such groups, some bishops have made use of their power to dispense from universal laws, which they enjoy under canon 87 §1 of the *Code of Canon Law*:

> Whenever he judges that it contributes to their spiritual welfare, the diocesan bishop can dispense the faithful from disciplinary laws, both universal laws and those particular laws made by the supreme ecclesiastical authority for his territory or his subjects. He cannot dispense from procedural laws or from penal laws, nor from those whose dispensation is specially reserved to the Apostolic See or to some other authority.

This canon in particular is a direct product of the Second Vatican Council, which established the corresponding principle in the Decree *Christus Dominus*.[102] It is one of the most notable changes introduced in the new *Code* as compared to the 1917 *Code*. Indeed, it reverses the previous rule whereby bishops exercised their power to dispense, not by virtue of a power of their own, but by virtue of five-year faculties granted by pontifical concession. Under this system, only the supreme

---

[102] Second Vatican Council, Decree concerning the Pastoral Office of Bishops in the Church *Christus Dominus*, October 28, 1965, no. 8b: "The general law of the Church grants the faculty to each diocesan bishop to dispense, in a particular case, the faithful over whom they legally exercise authority as often as they judge that it contributes to their spiritual welfare, except in those cases which have been especially reserved by the supreme authority of the Church."

authority could dispense universal laws (since it alone had established them); however, for practical reasons, Ordinaries would be granted multiple dispensation faculties. In place of this system of faculties, the new *Code* put in place a system of reservations whereby diocesan bishops may dispense from all laws, except those which the supreme authority has reserved to itself. The new Canon better reflects the doctrine, recalled at Vatican II, that bishops are not vicars of the pope, but rather vicars of Christ for their particular Church, over which they exercise "a proper, ordinary and immediate power," always under the authority of the pope.[103] It also reflects a less normativistic understanding of dispensations, whereby these are not *per se* reserved to the author of the law, but rather belong to the executive authority.

Under canon 87 §1, therefore, there is nothing to prevent a diocesan bishop from dispensing, for the good of the faithful, from certain provisions of *TC*, in particular from article 3 §2, which prohibits celebrations in parish churches. Indeed (and to use the words of *Evangelii Gaudium*), bishops are in a better position than the pope to discern the problems that arise in their territories.

---

[103] See Vatican II, *Lumen Gentium*, no. 27: "This power, which they personally exercise in Christ's name, is proper, ordinary and immediate, although its exercise is ultimately regulated by the supreme authority of the Church, and can be circumscribed by certain limits, for the advantage of the Church or of the faithful."

However, the CDW does not see things that way. The *Responsa* state:

> This Congregation, exercising the authority of the Holy See in matters within its competence (cf. *Traditionis Custodes*, n. 7), can grant, at the request of the diocesan bishop, that the parish church be used to celebrate according to the *Missale Romanum* of 1962 only if it is established that it is impossible to use another church, oratory, or chapel. The assessment of this impossibility must be made with the utmost care.

In other words, the Dicastery expressly reserves to itself the right to dispense with this provision of the motu proprio. But can it do so? This seems doubtful, since the bishops' right to dispense is part of universal law (can. 87 §1 *CIC*), and only the supreme legislator can limit it. And to support its claim, the Congregation simply invokes article 7 of *TC*, which grants it competencies of an administrative, rather than a legislative, nature. It would therefore seem that the principle of legality is not respected.

Non-Respect of the Principle of Legality

In administrative canon law, the principle of legality means, simply put, that ecclesiastical authority is subject to the law. Ecclesiastical administration must exercise its powers within its own limits and with due regard for the norms that have been legitimately established. It is quite incompetent in matters which pertain to the legislative and judicial powers. Even within its own area of competence, it must respect general principles of law, the fundamental rights of the faithful, and the legitimate autonomy of lower realities. We have seen that the CDW seems to disregard the rightful autonomy of the ex-*Ecclesia Dei* institutes, and that on at least two points it unduly encroaches on the rights of diocesan bishops, against universal law. Unfortunately, the principle of legality appears to be abused by the *Responsa* on several other points as well.

For example, whereas canon 902 sets forth the universal norm for concelebration as being a freedom of the priest,[104] the *Responsa* seem to make concelebration at the Chrism Mass a "necessary requirement in order to benefit from the concession to celebrate with the *Missale Romanum* of 1962."

Similarly, whereas canon 905 §2 provides that "If there is a scarcity of priests, the local Ordinary may for a good reason allow priests to celebrate twice in one day or even, if pastoral need requires it, three times on Sundays or holydays of obligation," the *Responsa* exclude this possibility when the Missal used is that of 1962: "It is not possible to grant bination, on the grounds that there is no 'just cause' or 'pastoral necessity' as required by canon 905 §2: the right of the faithful to the celebration of the Eucharist is in no way denied, since they are

---

[104] See Louis-Marie de Blignières, F.S.V.F., "À propos de la concélébration," in *Sedes Sapientiæ* 158 (December 2021): 9–11.

offered the possibility of participating in the Eucharist in its current ritual form."

This decision of the CDW not only unduly restricts local Ordinaries' faculties, substituting itself for the latter in discerning what is a just cause and what is not, but also shows little regard for the fundamental right of the faithful to follow their own rite and spirituality (cf. can. 214).

The Lack of a *Vacatio Legis*

Finally, one aspect of the new provisions which has not failed to surprise canonists[105] is the lack of a *vacatio legis*, i.e., a period of time between the promulgation of the law and its coming into force. This kind of delay is normal and easily understood. For a law to come into force immediately carries a risk of juridical insecurity (laws are made to last, not to change unexpectedly and overnight) and poses serious practical difficulties: the recipient community generally does not have time to study and understand the new provisions, nor to adapt to them. For this reason, the *Code of Canon Law* provides that laws are immediately binding only when the very nature of things requires it (cf. can. 8: "*nisi ex natura rei illico ligent*"). This would be the case, for example,

---

[105] See, for example, the reflections of Raymond Leo Cardinal Burke, former Prefect of the Supreme Tribunal of the Apostolic Signatura: "The Wonderful Gift of the *Usus Antiquior*," in Kwasniewski, ed., *From Benedict's Peace to Francis's War*, 114–20, also online at www.cardinalburke.com/presentations/traditionis-custodes.

with laws which are purely declarative of divine law (since divine law obliges regardless of its declaration by a human law), or with laws which merely acknowledge a custom or confirm some pre-existing law (such as authentic interpretations, which merely declare the sense of words that are certain in themselves: cf. can. 16 §2). Certainly, the *Code* gives the legislator a certain latitude to lengthen or reduce (but not eliminate) the *vacatio legis*. However canonists consider that such reduction of the time period can usually be justified only by some need to act quickly in order to put an end to a dangerous situation. And even in such a case, it must be a matter of norms that do not pose technical problems and, above all, do not prejudice acquired rights. In any case, as observed by Professor Baura, "the reduction of the *vacatio* cannot be arbitrary, but, since it is itself a legislative provision, it must also always be rational, respectful of the rights of those to whom the law is addressed."[106]

In the case of *TC*, which considerably restricts the rights of the faithful and which also contains a number of provisions that are unclear or difficult to apply (to say the least), good and prudent legislative practice would have been to provide for a fairly long *vacatio legis*.[107] However, this is not at all what the supreme legislator decided, since he even decided to suppress the *vacatio*

---

[106] Eduardo Baura, "Profili giuridici dell'arte di legiferare nella Chiesa," in *Ius Ecclesiae* XIX/1 (2007): 36.

[107] By way of comparison, the motu proprio *Summorum Pontificum* of July 7, 2007, which, far from restricting the rights of the faithful, rather declared them, did not come into force until the following September 14, in order to give those

altogether, ordering that the *motu proprio* come into force on the very day of its publication in *L'Osservatore Romano*. Again, this provision has already posed great problems, which were bound to lead, on the part of those to whom it was addressed, to non-compliance with, or even disregard for, the law.[108]

[See *Addendum 3*, p. 104]

---

to whom it was addressed the time to study the new provisions and to prepare themselves for their proper reception.

[108] Immediately after the publication of *Traditionis Custodes*, it was clear that art. 3 §2, which forbids public celebrations according to the *usus antiquior* in parish churches, is inapplicable in many countries where there are almost *exclusively* parish churches. Many diocesan bishops—before the *Responsa* were published—had to dispense from this provision under canon 87 §1. Others made no formal decision, letting Masses take place in an apparent illegality, in keeping with the axiom *ad impossibilia nemo tenetur* (no one is bound to do the impossible). This is a good example of the non-acceptance of an irrational legislative provision.

4

The Future of *Traditionis Custodes*

The normative apparatus introduced by *TC* and the *Responsa* appears defective in several respects, inconsistent with the rest of the canonical legal system, and little respectful of the rights of the faithful. It raises more doubts and difficulties than it solves. Above all, it lacks rationality, understood as adequacy with the reality that it claims to regulate—a reality no less than the fact of the existence, in the Church, of a centuries-old Roman Rite, substantially different from the modern rite produced by the liturgical reform of Paul VI. The former rite conveys a spirituality, practices, and methods of apostolate and evangelization of its own. Hundreds of thousands of lay faithful throughout the world, thousands of priests, seminarians, and religious men and women, feel attached to this rite. Institutes have been founded and canonically recognized on the basis of their permanent and exclusive attachment to this rite. It cannot be abrogated and will not disappear. It will remain alive *in sinu Ecclesiae*, as an irreplaceable richness of the Latin tradition and a bulwark of doctrinal orthodoxy.

What, then, will be the future of *TC*? The history of canon law, even in recent times, does not lack examples of laws that quickly fell into disuse because they were not adequate to the social reality they were intended to order.[109] However, the posterity of this motu proprio could well be unexpected. Insofar as it seems to ratify the abandonment of the vocabulary of "two forms of the Roman Rite," it could paradoxically constitute an important step towards the canonical recognition of two Latin rites in their own right, namely the "Roman" rite and the "modern" rite. Should this reality, albeit totally unprecedented, be fully taken into account by the legislator, and given the fact that "all legitimately recognized rites are equal in right and dignity" (cf. *SC* 4), the logical consequence would be the erection of personal ecclesiastical circumscriptions enjoying

---

[109] The most emblematic example of such non-acceptance—a true textbook example—is that of the Apostolic Constitution *Veterum Sapientia* of February 22, 1962, signed with great solemnity by John XXIII on the very altar of St. Peter's Confession, and which intended to promote the study and use of Latin in the Church. We know what happened thereafter. The massive abandonment of the Latin language in the postconciliar liturgy led to its virtual disappearance in the Church as a whole—so much so that many legislative texts today no longer have an original Latin text, a situation that is not free from serious difficulties, as we have seen throughout this study.

the faculty of celebrating all liturgical actions according to the traditional Roman Rite.[110]

These would certainly not be *sui iuris* Churches, such as those created for those Oriental communities which, from the sixteenth century onwards, entered into communion with the Roman Catholic Church. *Sui iuris* Churches are not normally chosen according to a subjective criterion (such as free personal choice); rather, they are local Churches which have an objective criterion of membership (baptism).[111] However, incorporation into such

---

[110] Fr. Donneaud at least considers the theoretical possibility of this, even if he finds it difficult to imagine (cf. "Le pape François, garant de la doctrine liturgique de saint Pius V," 50, n19).

[111] This was emphasized by Cardinal Ratzinger: "I am in *this* local Church, and I do not look for my friends there, I find my brothers and my sisters; and these brothers and sisters are not people we look for, we just find them there. This situation of the non-arbitrariness of the Church in which I find myself, which is not a church of my choice but rather the Church that presents itself to me, is a very important principle. It seems to me that the letters of St. Ignatius [of Antioch] run very strongly alone these lines: that this bishop is the Church; this is not my choice, as if I were to go with this or that group of friends; I am in the common Church, along with the poor, the wealthy, with people I like and people I do not like, with intellectuals and uneducated people; I am in the Church, which was there before me. Opening up the opportunity of choosing one's Church '*à la carte*' is something that could genuinely damage the structure of the Church" ("Assessment and Future Prospects," in *Collected Works*, 11:564). Nevertheless, it should be noted that can. 372 §2 *CIC* leaves open the possibility of erecting personal particular Churches: "If . . . in the judgement of the supreme authority in the Church, after consultation with the Episcopal Conferences concerned, it is thought to be helpful, there may be established in a given territory particular Churches distinguished by the rite of the faithful or by some other similar quality."

structures could take place not only on the basis of baptism, but also by voluntary membership, without the requirement of a dispensation from ecclesiastical authority (as is required for the transfer from one *sui iuris* Church to another; cf. can. 112 §1, 1 *CIC* and can. 36 *CCEO*); leaving the structure could take place in a similar fashion.[112] In addition, groups of faithful who would join such hierarchical communities would belong to the Latin Church. As such, they would remain subject to the *Code of Canon Law*, with due regard for the special discipline enjoyed by their hierarchical community.

These would therefore be hierarchical communities that are complementary to Dioceses, as described by the Congregation for the Doctrine of the Faith in the Letter *Communionis Notio*:

> For a more complete vision of this aspect of ecclesial com-
> munion—unity in diversity—one needs to bear in mind
> that there are institutions and communities established
> by the Apostolic Authority for specific pastoral tasks.

---

[112] This system of voluntary membership is already the case with the personal Apostolic Administration of St. John Mary Vianney of Campos, Brazil. See Congregation for Bishops, Decree of Erection of the Personal Apostolic Administration of St. John Mary Vianney *Animarum Bonum*, January 18, 2002, in *AAS* 94 (2002): 307, art. IX §1: "[The lay faithful] who, recognizing that they adhere to the particularities of this personal Apostolic Administration, ask to be part of it, must manifest their will in writing and their names will be entered in a register which must be kept at the headquarters of the Apostolic Administration. §2: There should also be entered into this register those who at the present time belong to this Apostolic Administration and those who are baptized into it."

They belong *as such* to the universal Church, though their members are also members of the particular Churches where they live and work. The manner of belonging to the particular Churches, with its own particular *flexibility*, takes different juridical forms. But it does not erode the unity of the particular Church founded on the bishop; rather, it helps endow this unity with the interior diversification which is a feature of *communion*.[113]

Whatever legal form might be chosen (prelature, ordinariate, apostolic administration), these would be personal ecclesiastical circumscriptions, with a pastor, a presbyterate, and a *coetus fidelium*. The Ordinaries who would head these hierarchical communities would be invested with the episcopal dignity, in order to be able to perform all the functions foreseen in the *Pontificale Romanum*. They would have their own jurisdiction, *cumulative* with that of the diocesan bishop. In this way, the faithful, even if they participate in ecclesial life almost exclusively within the complementary community, would remain members of the particular Church of their domicile or quasi-domicile, to whose services they could always have recourse. Experience has shown that these complementary hierarchical communities,[114] far from

---

[113] Congregation for the Doctrine of the Faith, Letter *Communionis Notio* on Some Aspects of the Church Understood as Communion, May 28, 1992, no. 16, in *AAS* 85 (1993): 847–48.

[114] To date, in addition to the aforementioned personal apostolic administration of St. John Mary Vianney of Campos, the Church has Military Ordinariates

being a danger to the unity of the local Church, represent for the latter a powerful means of evangelization.

In this way, a liturgical, theological, spiritual, and disciplinary patrimony would be fully recognized within the Latin Church, expressing its own way of living the one Catholic faith, and contributing powerfully to the salvation of souls. Should this be the fruit of *TC*, then it should be acknowledged that this controversial text would have had its rightful place in the plan of Providence. Is it not said of God that he writes straight with crooked lines?

(governed by the Apostolic Constitution *Spirituali Militum Curae* of April 21, 1986), Ordinariates for the Eastern Rite faithful in Latin territories, personal Ordinariates for Anglicans who have returned to full communion (Apostolic Constitution *Anglicanorum Coetibus*, November 4, 2009), and the personal prelature of *Opus Dei* (Apostolic Constitution *Ut Sit* of November 28, 1982).

Bibliography

Ecclesiastical Documents[115]

CANON LAW
Code of Canon Law (1917).
Code of Canon Law (1983).
Code of Canons of the Eastern Churches (1990).

POPES
Benedict XVI. Homily at Mass of Possession of the Chair of the Bishop of Rome. May 7, 2005.

———. Post-Synodal Apostolic Exhortation *Sacramentum Caritatis*. February 22, 2007.

———. Apostolic Letter *Summorum Pontificum*. July 7, 2007.

---

[115] Listed chronologically by document.

———. *Con Grande Fiducia*, Letter to bishops accompanying *Summorum Pontificum*. July 7, 2007.

———. Apostolic Constitution *Anglicanorum Coetibus*. November 4, 2009.

Francis. Apostolic Exhortation *Evangelii Gaudium*. November 24, 2013.

———. Apostolic Letter *Mitis Iudex Dominus Jesus*. August 15, 2015.

———. Apostolic Constitution *Episcopalis Communio*. September 15, 2018.

———. Apostolic Letter issued *motu proprio* on the Pontifical Commission *Ecclesia Dei*. January 17, 2019.

———. Apostlolic Letter *Authenticum Charismatis*. November 1, 2020.

———. Apostolic Letter *Traditionis Custodes*, with accompanying letter to bishops. July 16, 2021.

———. Apostolic Constitution *Praedicate Evangelium*. March 19, 2022.

John XXIII. Apostolic Constitution *Veterum Sapientia*. February 22, 1962.

———. *Gaudet Mater Ecclesia*. Address on the Occasion of the Solemn Opening of the Most Holy [Second Vatican] Council. October 11, 1962.

John Paul II. Apostolic Constitution *Scripturarum Thesaurus*. April 25, 1979.

———. Apostolic Constitution *Ut Sit*. November 28, 1982.

———. Apostolic Constitution *Spirituali Militum Curae*. April 21, 1986.

———. Apostolic Constitution *Pastor Bonus*. June 28, 1988.

———. Apostolic Letter *Ecclesia Dei Adflicta*. July 2, 1988.

———. Apostolic Constitution *Fidei Depositum*. October 11, 1992.

Paul VI. Apostolic Constitution *Sacram Liturgiam*. January 25, 1964.

———. Apostolic Constitution *Missale Romanum*. April 3, 1969.

———. Address at the General Audience. November 19, 1969.

———. Address at the General Audience. November 26, 1969.

———. *Allocutio in aula consistoriali palatii apostolici Vaticani.* May 24, 1976.

Pius XII. Allocution to the Assisi Liturgical Congress. September 22, 1956.

Trent, Council of. Session 22, Doctrine on the Most Holy Sacrifice of the Mass. September 17, 1562.

Vatican II. Constitution on the Sacred Liturgy *Sacrosanctum Concilium*. December 4, 1963.

———. Dogmatic Constitution on the Church *Lumen Gentium*. November 21, 1964.

———. Decree concerning the Pastoral Office of Bishops in the Church *Christus Dominus*. October 28, 1965.

ROMAN CURIA

Sacred Congregation for Divine Worship. Instruction *Memoriale Domini*. May 29, 1969.

Sacred Congregation for Divine Worship. *Notificatio De Missali romano, liturgia horarum et calendario*. June 14, 1971.

Sacred Congregation for Divine Worship. Circular Letter *Quattuor Abhinc Annos*. October 3, 1984.

Congregation for the Doctrine of the Faith. Letter *Communionis Notio.* May 28, 1992.

Secretariat of State. *Regolamento Generale della Curia Romana.* April 30, 1999.

Congregation for Bishops. Decree of Erection of the Personal Apostolic Administration of St. John Mary Vianney *Animarum Bonum.* January 18, 2002.

International Theological Commission. *Synodality in the Life and Mission of the Church.* March 2, 2018. www.vatican.va/roman_curia/congregations/cfaith/cti_documents/rc_cti_20180302_sinodalita_en.html.

Congregation for Divine Worship and the Discipline of the Sacraments. *Responsa ad Dubia.* December 4, 2021.

Other Sources

Anon. "Some Notes on the Congregation for Divine Worship's *Responsa ad Dubia* in light of Canon Law." *The Latin Mass Society of England & Wales.* December 21, 2021. Available at https://lms.org.uk/sites/default/files/u8/cdw_responsa_dec21.pdf.

Araña, José Antonio. "*Motu proprio.*" In *Diccionario General de Derecho Canónico*, ed. J. Otaduy, A. Viana, J. Sedano, vol. 5. Cizur Menor/Navarra: Editorial Aranzadi, 2012.

Arrieta, Juan Ignacio. "Sinodalità e sinodo dei vescovi." *Ius Ecclesiæ* 31/1 (2019): 275–88.

Aubry, Augustin-Marie, F.S.V.F. *Obéir ou assentir? De la "soumission religieuse" au magistère simplement authentique.* Paris: Desclée De Brouwer, 2015.

Baura, Eduardo. *Parte generale del diritto canonico. Diritto e sistema normativo.* Rome: EDUSC, 2013.

———. "Profili giuridici dell'arte di legiferare nella Chiesa." *Ius Ecclesiae* XIX/1 (2007): 13–36.

Boni, Geraldina. *La recente attività normativa ecclesiale: finis terræ per lo* ius canonicum? *Per una valorizzazione del ruolo del Pontificio Consiglio per i testi legislativi e della scienza giuridica nella Chiesa.* Modena: Mucchi Editore, 2021.

Bortoli, Federico. *La distribution de la communion dans la main. Études historiques, canoniques et pastorales.* Perpignan: Artège, 2019.

Bouyer, Louis. *Memoirs.* Translated by John Pepino. Kettering, OH: Angelico Press, 2015.

Bricout, Hélène, ed. *Du bon usage des normes en liturgie. Approche théologique et spirituelle après Vatican II.* Paris: Cerf, 2019.

Burke, Cardinal Raymond Leo. "The Wonderful Gift of the *Usus Antiquior.*" In *From Benedict's Peace to Francis's War*, ed. Peter Kwasniewski, 114–20. Brooklyn, NY: Angelico Press, 2021.

Calmel, Roger-Thomas, O.P. "Réparation publique au canon romain outragé." *Itinéraires* 206 (Sept.-Oct. 1976): 101–81.

Castillón-Hoyos, Cardinal Dario. "Risposte del Cardinale Presidente della Pontificia Commissione 'Ecclesia Dei' a certi quesiti." www.clerus.org/clerus/dati/2008-10/24-20/castrillon_rispost.html.

Condon, Ed. "Roche's Rules: Does the new Extraordinary Form instruction line up with Vatican II?" *The Pillar*, December 20, 2021. www.pillarcatholic.com/roches-rules-does-the-new-extraordinary.

Congar, Yves Marie-Joseph, O.P. *Le concile de Vatican II. Son Église, Peuple de Dieu et Corps du Christ.* Paris: Beauchesne, 1984.

———. *La Tradition et la vie de l'Église.* Paris: Fayard, 1963.

———. *Sainte Église. Études et approches ecclésiologiques.* Paris: Cerf, 1963.

Cupich, Blase. Policy of the Archdiocese of Chicago for Implementing *Traditionis Custodes*, December 25, 2021. www.chicago-catholic.com/chicagoland/-/article/2022/01/05/archdiocese-sets-policy-for-implementing-traditionis-custodes-.

de Blignières, Louis-Marie, F.S.V.F. "À propos de la concélébration." *Sedes Sapientiæ* 158 (December 2021): 9–11.

———. "The Pope and the Law of Religious Institutes." *Sedes Sapientiae* Special English-language Issue (2022): 15–19.

da Silveira, Arnaldo Xavier. *Two Timely Issues: The New Mass and the Possibility of a Heretical Pope.* Translated by John Russell Spann and José Aloisio Schelini. Spring Grove, PA: The Foundation for a Christian Civilization, 2022.

Davies, Michael. *Pope Paul's New Mass.* Kansas City, MO: Angelus Press, 2009.

de Mattei, Roberto. "Reflections on the Liturgical Reform." In *Looking Again at the Question of the Liturgy with Cardinal Ratzinger*, ed. Alcuin Reid, 130–44. Farnborough, UK: St. Michael's Abbey Press, 2003.

de Magistris, Cristiana de Magistris. "An Act of Weakness." In *From Benedict's Peace to Francis's War*, ed. Peter Kwasniewski, 180–83. Brooklyn, NY: Angelico Press, 2021.

Diradourian, Thomas, ed. *Laudate. Missel grégorien des fidèles.* Perpignan: Artège, 2021.

Donneaud, Henry, O.P. "Le pape François garant de la doctrine liturgique de saint Pie V." *Nouvelle revue théologique* 144 (Jan.-March 2022): 38–54.

Errázuriz, Carlos José. "Positivismo jurídico." In *Diccionario General de Derecho Canónico*, ed. J. Otaduy, A. Viana, J. Sedano, vol. 6.

Fiedrowicz, Michael. *The Traditional Mass. History, Form, and Theology of the Classical Roman Rite.* Translated by Rose Pfeifer. Brooklyn, NY: Angelico Press, 2020.

Fortescue, Adrian. *The Mass: A Study of the Roman Liturgy.* London: Longmans, Green & Co., 1913.

Gamber, Klaus. *The Reform of the Roman Liturgy: Its Problems and Background.* Translated Klaus D. Grimm. Fort Collins, CO: Roman Catholic Books, n.d.

Gélineau, Joseph, S.J. *Demain la liturgie. Essai sur l'évolution des assemblées chrétiennes.* Paris: Cerf, 1976.

Gromier, Léon. "La Semaine Sainte restaurée." *Opus Dei* 2 (1962): 76–90.

———. "Simples réflexions sur des choses restaurées." *Opus Dei* 5 (1961): 248–54.

Hazell, Matthew. "'All the Elements of the Roman Rite'? Mythbusting, Part II." *New Liturgical Movement*, October 1, 2021, www.newliturgicalmovement.org/2021/10/all-elements-of-roman-rite-mythbusting.html.

Joy, John P. *Disputed Questions on Papal Infallibility.* Lincoln, NE: Os Justi Press, 2022.

Kwasniewski, Peter, ed. *From Benedict's Peace to Francis's War: Catholics Respond to the Motu Proprio* Traditionis Custodes *on the Latin Mass.* Brooklyn, NY: Angelico Press, 2021.

————. *Holy Bread of Eternal Life: Restoring Eucharistic Reverence in an Age of Impiety*. Manchester, NH: Sophia Institute Press, 2020.

————. "'O, What a Tangled Web…': Thirty-Three Falsehoods in the CDW's *Responsa ad Dubia*." *OnePeterFive*, January 5, 2022. https://onepeterfive.com/thirty-three-falsehoods -responsa.

————. *The Once and Future Roman Rite: Returning to the Traditional Latin Liturgy after Seventy Years of Exile*. Gastonia, NC: TAN Books, 2022.

————. *True Obedience in the Church: A Guide to Discernment in Challenging Times*. Manchester, NH: Sophia Institute Press, 2021.

Lucien, Bernard. "The Magisterial Authority of Vatican II." *Sedes Sapientiæ*, Special English-language Issue (2022): 21–90.

Madiran, Jean. *Histoire de la messe interdite*. Versailles: Via Romana, 2009.

Maugendre, Jean-Pierre, et al. *Bref examen critique de la communion dans la main*. Versailles: Contretemps, 2021.

Montagna, Diane. "Guarding the Flock: A Canon Lawyer's Advice to Bishops on Latest Vatican Crackdown on Tradition." Interview with Fr Gerald Murray. February 15, 2022. https:// remnantnewspaper.com/web/index.php/articles/item/5851- the-future-of-the-latin-mass-a-canon-lawyer-s-take-on -traditionis-custodes.

Ottaviani, Cardinal Alfredo, with Cardinal Antonio Bacci. *Short Critical Study of the New Order of Mass ("The Ottaviani Intervention")*. Translated by Anthony Cekada. West Chester, OH: Philothea Press, 2010.

Parise, Giovanni. "Soppressione di una parrocchia e impossibilità di sanare un atto amministrativo illegittimo da parte del superiore gerarchico." *Ius Ecclesiæ* XXXIII/1 (2021): 241–74.

Pietrzyk, Pius, O.P. "A Dominican Canonist Responds to the *Responsa ad Dubia.*" February 8, 2022. https://edwardpentin.co.uk/a-dominican-canonist-responds-to-the-responsa-ad-dubia.

Prétot, Patrick, O.S.B. "La réforme de la semaine sainte sous Pie XII (1951–1955). Enjeux d'un premier pas vers la réforme liturgique de Vatican II." *Questions liturgiques* 93 (2012): 196–217.

Pristas, Lauren. "Theological Principles of the Roman Missal (1970)." *The Thomist* 67 (2003): 157–95.

Ratzinger, Joseph. Letter to Professor Wolfgang Waldstein, Regensburg, December 14, 1976. Original German text in "Zum motu proprio *Summorum Pontificum,*" *Una Voce Korrespondenz* 38/3 (2008): 201–14.

———. *Milestones: Memoirs 1927–1977.* Translated by Erasmo Leiva-Merikakis. San Francisco: Ignatius Press, 1998.

———. "Ten Years of the Motu Proprio *Ecclesia Dei.*" Lecture given by Cardinal Ratzinger at the Ergife Palace Hotel, Rome, October 24, 1998; in *Adoremus Bulletin*, December 31, 2007, https://adoremus.org/2007/12/ten-years-of-the-motu-proprio-quotecclesia-deiquot.

———. *Theology of the Liturgy.* Edited by Michael J. Miller. *Collected Works*, volume 11. San Francisco: Ignatius Press, 2014.

Reid, Alcuin, ed. *Looking Again at the Question of the Liturgy with Cardinal Ratzinger*. Farnborough, UK: St. Michael's Abbey Press, 2003.

———. *The Organic Development of the Liturgy*. Second edition. San Francisco: Ignatius Press, 2005.

Rivoire, Réginald-Marie, F.S.V.F. *La valeur doctrinale de la discipline canonique*. Rome: EDUSC, 2016.

Roguet, Aimon-Marie, O.P. *Table ouverte. La messe d'aujourd'hui*. Paris: Desclée, 1969.

Salleron, Louis. *La nouvelle messe*. Second edition. Paris: NEL, 1976.

Sánchez Gil, Antonio. "Gli innovativi profili canonici del motu proprio *Summorum Pontificum* sull'uso della Liturgia romana anteriore alla riforma del 1970." *Ius Ecclesiæ* XIX (2007): 689–708.

Santos, Manoel Augusto. "Sinodalidad." In *Diccionario General de Derecho Canónico*, ed. J. Otaduy, A. Viana, J. Sedano, vol. 7. Cizur Menor/Navarra: Editorial Aranzadi, 2012.

Shaw, Joseph. "*Responsa ad dubia*: good news on private Masses." *LMS Chairman*, December 27, 2021. www.lmschairman. org/2021/12/responsa-ad-dubia-good-news-on-private.html.

Stickler, Cardinal Alfons. "Recollections of a Vatican II Peritus." *New Liturgical Movement*, June 29, 2022, www.newliturgicalmovement.org/2022/06/recollections-of-vatican-ii-peritus -by.html.

Thomas Aquinas. *Summa theologiae*. Translated by Fr. Laurence Shapcote, O.P. Latin/English Edition of the Works of St. Thomas Aquinas. Green Bay, WI: Aquinas Institute; Steubenville, OH: Emmaus Academic, 2012.

About the Author

~⁓~

Fr. Réginald-Marie Rivoire, of the Fraternity of St. Vincent Ferrer, graduated from the *Institut d'Etudes Politiques* of Paris and holds a doctorate in canon law (Pontifical University of the Holy Cross, Rome). He is the Master of Novices at the Friary of St. Thomas Aquinas in Chémeré-le-Roi, France, and Defender of the Bond and Promoter of Justice at the ecclesiastical Tribunal of Rennes, France. He teaches canon law in various religious institutes. His latest publication is "La situation juridique de la communion dans la main," in *Bref examen critique de la communion dans la main* (Versailles: Contretemps, 2021).

Addendum 1
(see page 61)

The abandonment of this terminology is well confirmed by the correction *in extremis* of the apostolic constitution *Prædicate Evangelium.* While the text made public on March 19, 2022 still stated in Article 93 that "the Dicastery [for Divine Worship] is concerned with the regulation and discipline of the Sacred Liturgy with regard to the Extraordinary Form of the Roman Rite," the Holy See announced on March 21, at a press conference presenting the document, that this was "a typo that needed to be corrected. The new article 93 reads: 'The Dicastery is concerned with the regulation and discipline of the sacred liturgy with regard to the use—granted according to the established norms—of liturgical books prior to the reform of the Second Vatican Council.'" It is astonishing that a legislative text of such importance—an apostolic constitution—should be corrected at the last moment, after already having been made public. Canonists will naturally see this as a further illustration of the legislative anarchy that is rampant in the present pontificate. It should also be noted that this very solemn document confirms the perenniality of the traditional liturgy, since it admits the possibility of using the liturgical books prior to the reform, even though they would no longer be (according to article 1 of *TC*) an expression of the *lex orandi* of the Latin rite. Let him understand who can . . .

Addendum 2
(*see page 67*)

Clearly, it did not occur to the supreme legislator that there might be an inconsistency here. In any case, it seems he is not averse to contradictions. In a "decree" dated February 11, 2022, that is, less than two months after the publication of the *Responsa ad dubia*, the pope himself recognized that the Priestly Fraternity of St. Peter was not affected by the new norms. With this decree, the Pope "concedes . . . to each and every member" of this society of apostolic life "the faculty of celebrating the sacrifice of the Mass, of administering the sacraments and other sacred rites, and of performing the Divine Office, according to the typical editions of the liturgical books in force in the year 1962, that is to say, the Missal, the Ritual, the Pontifical and the Roman Breviary."[116]

Formally, this *decretum* is a particular administrative act, in this case a rescript granting to certain persons (juridical and physical) a favor *contra vel præter legem communem*: what in technical terms is called a privilege (cf. can. 76).[117] Some commentaries

---

[116] Original Latin text available on the website of the Fraternity of St. Peter: https://www.fssp.org/fr/decretum/.

[117] In canon law, the term "privilege" does not have the pejorative connotation of "unjust favor" that it has in secular law. Privilege is always an instrument of justice, which does not harm the common good—the *salus animarum*—but on the contrary serves it, by means of the favor granted to a particular subject because of particular circumstances. Privilege, as recognized in canon law, is always and only just. Cf. Javier Canosa, "Privilegio," in *DGDC*, vol. VI, p. 473.

have therefore immediately emphasized the exceptional, gracious (it is an indult), and revocable (therefore precarious) character of the right granted.[118] A privilege can in fact always be revoked by the competent authority (cf. can. 79)—that is, either the one who granted the privilege or his successor.

However, this judgment must be qualified. On the one hand, unless one adopts a purely positivist view of the law, which would see in the privilege only a "*fait du prince*" [arbitrary government act], it is clear that the competent authority can revoke a privilege only for a proportionate and rational reason, respecting acquired rights and other requirements of justice. On the other hand, and without entering here into the much debated question of the juridical nature (administrative or legislative) of privilege, a topic on which canonists have long been divided,[119] it should be noted that a longstanding tradition sees privilege as a "private law granted with benevolent intent," and therefore as a particular norm, obligatory *erga omnes* [i.e., binding on everyone]. The notion of privilege is therefore not without affinity to that of law properly speaking.

If this decree of February 11, 2022 confirms the return to the approach of the "indult," by which the legislator had thought fit to regulate the liturgical question before *Summorum Pontificum*

---

[118] See, for example, the argument developed by the Priestly Society of St. Pius X on the website of its French district, *La Porte latine*: "The Price of Silence," February 24, 2022, https://laportelatine.org/formation/crise-eglise/ecclesiadeisme/le-prix-du-silence.

[119] For an overview of this historical debate, see Eduardo Labandeira, *Trattato di diritto amministrativo canonico* (Milan: Giuffrè, 1994), 327–49.

(and, as such, appears to be a real step backwards), it also signifies, on the part of the supreme legislator, a full recognition of the proper right of the Priestly Fraternity of St. Peter.[120] It is difficult to see how this recognition would not also apply to the institutes *ad instar* [after the fashion of], that is to say, to all those that formerly depended on the Pontifical Commission *Ecclesia Dei*.[121] The permanence of the special faculties granted is guaranteed by the proper law of the institute, which has received definitive approval. Granted in 1988 and recognized again in 2022, these *special* but *habitual* faculties are an integral element of the juridical status of these institutes and, as such, are perpetual.

At first glance, this recognition of proper law might seem limited, since it is valid, according to the terms of the decree, only "in the churches and oratories proper" to the institute. "Everywhere

---

[120] The word "concedes" in the decree should not be misinterpreted. An analysis of the text reveals—as was confirmed to us by the superiors of the FSSP who had requested this decree during a private audience with the Holy Father a few days earlier—that the text of the decree of February 11, 2022 is in fact a "copy and paste" of the decree of erection of the FSSP of October 18, 1988, by which the new society was granted the use of the ancient books. There is no new concession, but the simple recognition of an acquired right.

[121] See the *Official Communiqué of the Fraternity of St. Peter*, February 21, 2022 (www.fssp.fr/2022/02/21/communique-officiel-de-la-fraternite-sacerdotale-saint-pierre-2/): "During this audience, the Pope was particularly keen to make it clear that institutes such as the Fraternity of St. Peter were not affected by the general provisions of the motu proprio *Traditionis Custodes*, since the use of the ancient liturgical books was at the origin of their existence and provided for by their constitutions."

else, [the members] shall use this faculty [to follow the ancient books] only with the consent of the Ordinary of the place, except for the celebration of private Mass."

In reality, this incision is simply an application of canon 678 § 1 of the *Code of Canon Law*, which makes the members of institutes subject to the bishops for all "that which concerns the care of souls, the public exercise of divine worship, and other works of the apostolate." It should be remembered, however, that by virtue of the second paragraph of this same canon, *the local ordinary is himself bound to respect the discipline proper to the institute.* A bishop is perfectly free to accept or not to accept such and such an apostolic institute in his diocese; but once he *has* accepted it, he also necessarily accepts the fact that its members carry out in his diocese the apostolic works that correspond to the nature and specific purpose of the institute. The authorization to carry out these proper works is already included in the consent given by the bishop for the erection of the house of the institute (cf. can. 611, 2°). A bishop who has, in his diocese, a house of an apostolic institute formerly dependent on the Pontifical Commission Ecclesia Dei cannot, therefore, prohibit its members from exercising their apostolate in accordance with the charism of the institute—that is, by using the liturgical books prior to the postconciliar reform.

This decree of February 11, 2022, thus appears to be a matter of catching up: the legislator's belated consideration of what had been forgotten in the text of *TC* and passed over in silence by the *Responsa*, namely, the existence of institutes whose constitutions, definitively approved, provide for habitual, or even exclusive, celebration according to the liturgical books prior to the post-conciliar reform.[122]

Addendum 3

(see page 80)

A Case of "Patching-up":
The Rescript of Audience of February 20, 2023

These innumerable difficulties of application led the Cardinal Prefect of the Dicastery for Divine Worship to request from the Supreme Pontiff an "*oraculum vivæ vocis*" in order to "confirm" the provisions of the *Responsa*, which until then had been doubt-ful, not to say invalid. This *oraculum vivæ vocis* was attested to by a rescript of audience signed by the head of the dicastery on February 20, 2023 and made public the following day.[123]

---

[122] The final provision of the decree is somewhat perplexing: "Without prejudice to what has been said above, the Holy Father suggests that, as far as possible, the provisions of the motu proprio *Traditionis Custodes* should also be taken into account." On the one hand, the wishes and suggestions of the legislator should hardly have place in a text of a juridi-cal nature; on the other hand, it is difficult to see how the provisions of a general norm can be "taken into account" when they are contradicted by proper law.

[123] Original Italian text available on the Holy See website: www.vatican.va/roman_curia/congregations/ccdds/documents/rc_con_ccdds_doc_20230220_rescriptum-traditioniscustodes_it.html.

In itself, the procedure is not exceptional. The juridical figure of the *rescriptum ex audientia Sanctissimi* is well known to canonists. Audience rescripts are true pontifical acts that contain the oral decisions of the Roman Pontiff transmitted to the dicasteries of the Roman Curia. The prefect of the dicastery asks the pope for oral approval of a provision, which may be a general norm of a legislative nature. In drafting and signing the rescript of audience, which is a proof, the prefect acts as a notary. If the rescript contains a universal law, it must also be promulgated. Audience rescripts, whether they contain particular measures or general norms, have multiplied during the present pontificate, no doubt because they fit well with Pope Francis's personal manner of governing.

The rescript of audience of February 20, 2023, expressly reserves to the Holy See the dispensation of two provisions of *TC*, namely: (1) the use of a parish church or the erection of a personal parish for the celebration of the Eucharist according to the *Missale Romanum* of 1962; (2) the permission given to a priest ordained after July 16, 2021 to celebrate Mass according to that same missal.

Rather than a *confirmatio*, this new measure should be seen as a veritable *sanatio* of the provisions of the *Responsa* by which the Dicastery for Divine Worship had arrogated to itself such a reservation, in defiance of the principle of legality. With this rescript of audience, the Pope, as supreme legislator, thus ratifies the *Responsa* and decides that certain dispensations of the *TC* are indeed reserved to the Apostolic See. The rescript also states that the Roman Pontiff "confirms—after having already expressed his assent in the audience of November 18, 2021—that which was established in the *Responsa ad dubia*, together with the attached explanatory notes of December 4, 2021."

This new document, which is both a "turn of the screw" and a "patching-up," does not, however, solve all the problems; indeed, it even gives rise to new ones. We will limit ourselves to a few remarks.

First of all, from a formal point of view, if it is difficult not to see a pontifical law in this rescript restricting the faculty of dispensation of diocesan bishops, we observe that the pontifical approval is still not given *in forma specifica*, contrary to what is foreseen in article 126 § 4 of the *General Regulations of the Roman Curia* (RGCR). According to this article, the approval *in forma specifica*, by which the Roman Pontiff endorses the decision of the dicastery, must appear explicitly in the approved norm itself. This is not the case here. The Roman Pontiff, the supreme legislator, is certainly not obliged to comply with the RGCR, but it would be good legislative prudence for him to do so. The canonical rules for producing norms are relatively simple, especially when compared to State rules. Legislative activity in the Church remains subject to a minimum of formal requirements, which the legislator (or his delegate) should not readily dispense with, on pain of increasing legal uncertainty. The vicissitudes of the *Responsa ad dubia* are a good illustration of this truth.

As to its substance, this rescript of audience confirms the centralization of power that is one of the marks of Pope Francis's pontificate. While article 2 of *TC* claims to give back "to the diocesan bishop, as organizer, promoter, and guardian of the whole liturgical life in the particular Church entrusted to him" the care "to regulate the liturgical celebrations in his diocese," affirming that "it is his *exclusive competence* to authorize recourse to the 1962 *Missale Romanum* in his diocese," the rescript of February 20, 2023, in line with the *Responsa* of December 4, 2021, confirms that this episcopal freedom is to be exercised only in one direction: that of restricting celebrations according to the *Vetus Ordo*. The rescript represents a clear step backward from the advances of Vatican II (*Christus Dominus* 8b) recognizing the diocesan bishop's customary faculty of dispensing from universal laws. The bishop's ability to discern now becomes suspect when it is exercised in favor of expanding (or even maintaining) the possibilities of celebrating according to the ancient rite. The omniscient Dicastery for Divine Worship apparently knows better than the bishop does what is good for his particular diocese, nay, for such and such a parish, for such and such a community of the faithful, even for such and such a newly ordained priest!

This fussy grip of the Dicastery claims to be exercised even for *past* acts. The rescript states that "if a diocesan bishop has granted dispensations in the two cases mentioned above, he is obliged to inform the Dicastery for Divine Worship and the Discipline of the Sacraments, which will evaluate the individual cases." This sentence sounds like a thinly-veiled threat to call into question acquired rights, which are protected by the principle of non-retroactivity of juridical norms (cf. cann. 4 and 9).

Finally, in practice, it is likely that this rescript of audience will have only a very limited effect. This is so because, on the one hand, it does not concern "ex-*Ecclesia Dei*" institutes and, on the other hand, because the *Responsa* that were already inapplicable will not suddenly become so by a simple approval of the pope, as if by the wave of a magic wand. If we consider only the question of the place of celebration, the prohibition of celebrating in a parish church comes up against the reality that in many dioceses there are *only* parish churches, that is, churches that belong canonically to the juridical person of the parish. The diocesan bishops can certainly ask the dicastery for a dispensation, but if it is refused, they will have no other option than to tolerate a *de facto* situation. A juridical solution—possible when the parish has several churches, which is generally the case when it is the result of the regrouping of former parishes—would undoubtedly be to make one of them an "oratory" (can. 1223) or a "sanctuary" (can. 1230). The building then becomes what is called in some countries a "rectoral church." Finally, nothing prevents the diocesan bishop from authorizing the celebration of the traditional Mass in his own church, the cathedral.

This umpteenth document—people have spoken of a "piling up of norms," of a "waltz of decrees"—concerning the use of the traditional liturgy appears to be an admission of impotence on the part of the legislator. Regulative inflation is never a good sign. "*Corruptissima re publica plurimæ leges.*"[124]

---

[124] "The more numerous the laws, the more corrupt the state": Tacitus, *Annals*, Bk. III, ch. 27.

Os Justi Press specializes in reprinting Catholic classics and new works that support the Roman Church's traditional Faith. Check out some of our other titles:

DOGMATIC THEOLOGY
Lattey (ed.), *The Incarnation*
Lattey (ed.), *St Thomas Aquinas*
Pohle, *God: His Knowability, Essence, and Attributes*
Pohle, *The Author of Nature and the Supernatural*
Scheeben, *A Manual of Catholic Theology* (2 vols.)
Scheeben, *Nature and Grace*

SPIRITUAL THEOLOGY
Doyle, *Vocations*
Guardini, *Sacred Signs*
Leen, *The True Vine and Its Branches*
Swizdor, *God in Me*

LITURGY
The Life of Worship
A Benedictine Martyrology
The Roman Martyrology (Pocket Edition)
Chaignon, *The Sacrifice of the Mass Worthily Offered*
Croegaert, *The Mass: A Liturgical Commentary* (2 vols.)
Kwasniewski (ed.), *John Henry Newman on Worship, Reverence, and Ritual*
Parsch, *The Breviary Explained*
Pothier, *Cantus Mariales*

LANGUAGE & LITERATURE
The Little Flowers of Saint Francis (illustrated)
Brittain, *Latin in Church*
Farrow, *Pageant of the Popes*
Kilmer, *Anthology of Catholic Poets*
Walsh, *The Catholic Anthology*

www.ingramcontent.com/pod-product-compliance
Lightning Source LLC
Chambersburg PA
CBHW031434120626
46545CB00006B/2392